Tayteonna,

Prepare to Love

100 QUESTIONS AND ANSWERS

LEONARD L. ADAMS, JR.

May love always be your guide.. —

Leonard L. Adams Jr.

Relearning Love Press

Introduction

I had been so mercilessly abused and woefully neglected by my parents that, by the time I was a teenager, the last thing in the world I wanted to do was love anyone. I thought it felt good to let the hate course through what seemed to be the depths of my soul. In it seemed protection—the perfect place for anyone looking to peer into me to finally give up. Though it remained a place of never-ending pain, sadness, hopelessness, and anger, I thought it guaranteed me protection against any future pain.

When people tried to love me, I pushed them away. When I tried assuaging my loneliness with relationships, flashbacks of what it meant to love scared me so badly that I sabotaged those same relationships. The people I chose for relationships often faced the same demons, so it was inevitable that our togetherness would run its course.

Then I joined the U.S. Army at 20 years old and was trained as a counselor. The circumstances that led me to that field had nothing to do with the occupation itself or the grateful benefit I would derive from it. It had simply been a case of a biological deficit.

My older brother had joined the Army years before I considered it, and he talked me into doing the same. He was a nurse in the Army, and I wanted to follow suit. A few years before, I had entered college as the equivalent of a pre-med major (the college I attended didn't have a pre-med program as such, but I majored in Zoology with the intention of going to medical school afterwards, but I was too emotionally messed up to continue after my first year). I figured I would train as a nurse in the Army, then have the Army pay for me to go to medical school. I aced my test to join the Army and was about to enter Basic Training.

Upon reporting and choosing my vocation as a nurse, I was informed that I couldn't do so because I'm colorblind. I was crushed, but I remembered what my brother told me—if, for any reason, I couldn't be a nurse, make sure that I chose a job in the medical field. I searched the manual of Army medical jobs, and the first one I came across that didn't have a color vision requirement was the job as a Behavioral Science Specialist—what is known today as a mental health counselor.

Thus I became a counselor, and thus began my true guidance to real life.

It's tempting to see the world as a counselor in terms of us and them, as in they're the ones with the problems, and we're the ones with the solutions—especially as a young counselor. But I quickly realized that the tools I was given to help others were tools I could use to help myself.

Because I didn't trust anyone, thus making myself accountable to no one, the process of recovery was very slow, tedious, laborious, frustrating, and there were many times I lost hope. But it didn't take long for me to realize that this process was exactly what I needed, though at the time I wasn't sure why. For me, in the beginning, it was just a way to face and overcome the pain that I had called life. It was answers to all the whys I had. Over the decades, though, it became much more.

I began to realize that there were moments that shattered me, incident by incident, but that there were times before any of those incidents. Times when I wasn't afraid to love or be loved. Times before my heart was broken—times when my heart was whole. Granted, they were in very early childhood, but they existed. Even when the abuse and neglect began, I still yearned to love and be loved, but pain and disappointment slowly chipped away at hope, till all hope for being loved was lost. It became a self-fulfilled prophecy for me to keep people away, thus "proving" that I was unloved and, indeed, unlovable.

Understanding the need to forgive to regain my life and my power took decades. I thought that, reaching that place, I was whole.

But I wasn't.

I still spent additional decades denying myself the love I deserved from me while I worked to make others feel the love I wish I had. This still resulted in my feeling lonely, incomplete, angry at myself for not insisting on maintaining boundaries, and frustration at others for not loving me the way I loved them.

Then, over time, it slowly dawned on me like the beauty of nature that surrounds me unnoticed, decade after decade, until time, life, and circumstance conspire to create an epiphany out of what had been taken for granted, that I missed the most important part. The part where it all began. The part that had no question.

That part began with me—loving myself with a gentle tenderness, and from that love I was able to love others. Knowing, without being taught, that I was worthy, before cruelty convinced me I wasn't. Realizing that cruelty was wrong, and life was right. Cruelty lied to me, but love was my first teacher.

Thus was born my mission, Relearning Love.

This book takes 100 real-life questions from actual people and endeavors to bring us back to the self-love and self-worth we didn't have to be convinced of before we were talked out of it by the cruelties and pains of life and circumstances. The goal of this book (and others before and to follow) is to advocate for this *and* that, instead of this *or* that. Cruelties and pains have taught us so much, but the goal is to learn the lessons without the price being paid by love.

Healing from pain is beautiful, but the objective is to relearn how we loved before the pain while remembering the lessons pain taught us.

Contents

ONE

How do I respond to a breakup email?

I woke up to a breakup email this morning, saying,

"*I'm sorry, but we can't be together anymore. I've been doing a lot of thinking, and I just can't do it anymore. I love you and I think I always will, but I just can't do it. Everything I do makes you unhappy. Everywhere I go to is someplace you don't want me to. I just feel trapped. I can't wear makeup around any of my friends because you think I'm getting 'cute' for someone. I can't wear certain things because you think I'm showing off my butt or that everyone in the world will be staring at me. I can't be my own person and hang out with my friends without you getting mad. I'm just tired of it. I'm at that stage in my life right now where I want to be free and work on me and my job.*

"*Every fight we've gotten into lately has made me distance myself from you emotionally. I'm mentally detached from you. I don't feel connected to you. I don't wake up in the morning and crave talking to you like I used to. Our relationship has been toxic from the start. We 'communicate,' but it's hard when you don't understand or comprehend what I'm saying. How can you communicate when the other person doesn't understand?*

"I know everyone says you're supposed to work together and grow together in a relationship, but people need to normalize breaking up over these things. You deserve to be happy, get that money, live your life, hang out with your friends, etc., but I just don't feel it anymore. I don't. I don't want anyone else, but I want to be alone. I'm sorry, I am."

How do I respond to it?

Let me begin with an attempt to interpret what she's saying.

She feels emotionally exhausted and hopeless, because she believes she can't do anything to make you happy without sacrificing her own need to be happy. She doesn't feel safe with you, and she can't allow you to be her sanctuary. She thinks she must tiptoe around your feelings to be with you, and it causes her great anxiety.

The things she does simply for herself, such as the makeup or the clothes she wears or the friends she hangs out with, you insist she does for others or for attention. You refuse to listen to her, believing you know more about her motivations than she does when, in truth, you're projecting either your fears, your guilt, or both onto her, and if you're willing to admit it, you will realize you have no evidence that she is motivated for the reasons you say she is.

As she sees it, you make no attempt to understand her point of view or to see things as she sees them. **She must feel safe to connect with you, crave talking to you, crave *you*, or even want to be around you.** Every fight the two of you have had has made her lose even more faith that the relationship can work. She asks you this: why won't you *try* to understand me? "I'm worth it", she adds, "and for us to have a relationship, the relationship must be worth it for *me*. If you don't think I'm worth understanding, it isn't worth the attempt to save the relationship."

She goes on to wonder, since it's apparent that neither of you are happy, why do you insist on remaining unhappy by continuing in this relationship? Do you think you can manipulate her into being the person you want her to be so that you can be happy, with no concern for how she feels? Do you believe you know what she needs to be and do to be happy better than she does? Or do you even care if she's happy, as long as you are? Or that making you happy will, somehow, make *her* happy as well?

Now let's get to your question—how do you respond to this message from her? If you're asking how to respond to it for the purpose of winning her back, you've missed the point. Looking for a way to respond so that you can get what you want, without showing the same motivation for seeing her needs met, is a one-sided approach that will never permanently work, no matter how skillful, manipulative, or guilt-causing you are.

If you're asking how to respond for the purpose of her well-being, the best response is to show that you hear everything she's saying to you, and that the things that she's saying are more important than whether the relationship continues.

Are you willing to devote yourself entirely to her well-being in your response, with no expectation of reward? Is her peace of mind more important than the relationship? If you answered yes to both, then respond to her accordingly. If you responded no to one or both, it's best that you don't respond at all. Instead, walk away, learn the lessons you will from this relationship, and try your best not to let the things that made this relationship fail follow you to your next relationship. Take the time you need to grow, heal, and prepare for another relationship *before* starting a new one.

Two

How do I ask a woman on a date?

*O*K, *to start off, I am a guy in my early 20s. Never dated or anything like that. And to be completely honest, for most of my life except for the past year or so, I've had no interest to anyways. I always felt weirded out how women must deal with so much BS, seeing it firsthand from girls I've been friends with, as well as from my mom who raised me by herself. I always felt pressured to never tell a girl I knew I liked her or anything for fear of rejection, as well as any more unneeded BS I thought I would cause them by doing so.*

I guess the thing I'm really trying to ask is this. When do you feel comfortable asking a girl out on a date, or telling them you like them or something? I'm just genuinely curious, and I want to break out of the shell my fear keeps me in. But I never would want to scare away a person I've become friends with or something either by doing so. Any help would be appreciated.

Women have gone through horrible things because of men since the beginning (and vice versa), and the fact that you empathize with that means that you're less likely to be one of the ones doing this to them, so it's not something you should worry about doing.

Let me begin by saying that you may never be completely comfortable asking a woman out on a date, because rejection will always be a possibility. **A fear of rejection is one of the greatest fears we face, but one that can be successfully managed.**

Fear of rejection comes from the things we tell ourselves, and to manage it, we must change what we tell ourselves that causes the fear. Ask yourself this: what's the worst thing that'll happen if my request is rejected? How awful is it *really*? Will my world end? Or is it just unfortunate and disappointing? Because it's what you *tell* yourself about being rejected that causes your devastation. Stop thinking that others *must not* reject you or that your worth hinges on everyone accepting you. Instead, realize it's only a *preference*, not a *necessity*, that you never get rejected. It would be nice if things always went your way, right? But is that realistic? Is a preference a *law*, a *must*, a *have to*, or is it simply a preference? One of the greatest measures of freedom you'll ever experience is when you're **convinced** that not everyone will like you, and you're good with that! And keep in mind that a rejection of a request for a date is just that, a rejection of a request, not a rejection of you.

You may never be unafraid to ask a woman out, but you must decide to feel the fear and do it anyway, or it won't get done. Unless a woman sends clear, unambiguous signals that she likes you in that way, you may never feel comfortable, but it will never be a possibility if you don't ask.

Another thing you can do is figure out what scares you so much about asking a woman out on a date. There are situations that can make you feel nervous or insecure about dating, such as approaching a woman, making small talk, asking for her number, or suggesting a date. You can write down these triggers and rate them on a scale from 0 to 10, where 0 is no anxiety and 10 is extreme anxiety. This can help you become more aware of your fears and how they affect you.

Challenge the thoughts that sabotage your efforts for a date. These are irrational or exaggerated thoughts that make you doubt yourself or expect the worst, such as "She will reject me", "I'm not good enough for her", or "I'll make a fool of myself". You can write down these thoughts and evaluate them for evidence, logic, and helpfulness. You can also reframe them with more realistic and positive thoughts, such as "She might say yes", "I have many qualities that make me attractive", or "I can handle this situation". This can help you reduce your anxiety and increase your self-esteem.

Practice exposure. This is a technique where you gradually expose yourself to your dating anxiety triggers in a safe and controlled way. You can start with the least anxiety-provoking trigger and work your way up to the most anxiety-provoking one. For example, you can practice approaching a woman in a low stake setting, such as a bookstore or a coffee shop, and ask her for the time or a recommendation. You can then practice making small talk with her, asking for her number, or suggesting a date. You can also practice these scenarios in your imagination or with a friend before doing them in real life. This can help you overcome your fears and build your confidence.

The biggest thing, and it's huge, is to have no expectations when you ask. Remember that asking leaves room for both yes and no, not just yes.

THREE

My boyfriend won't forgive me unless I kneel and lick his feet.

*M*y boyfriend is very sensitive. It feels like I'm walking on eggshells all the time. I almost feel like I'm being emotionally abused. During the first stages of our relationship, he used to offend me a lot. He still does, and he writes it off by saying that those are facts, and I must face reality.

There were instances where I've said some harsh stuff in the heat of the moment and he would swear at me, call me names, and I had to beg for forgiveness. Once he demanded that he would forgive me if I knelt and licked his feet, which I wouldn't do, and he asked how I dare have the audacity to refuse when I've hurt him.

Recently, I commented on his career and laughed it off because it was a little teasing, but he won't believe that it was a joke. He blew up on me and said an apology wouldn't cut it. I've apologized multiple times, and he won't budge. I don't expect him to forgive me instantly like I do him, but going this far is ridiculous. He says the only way he'll feel better *is by taking revenge on me. He expects me to get on all fours and lick his feet and only then will he forgive me. I don't know why, but I verbally agreed to it. I haven't seen him yet, so I haven't done it—I only agreed to do it. He told me the reason he's acting this way is because I've hurt him many times and I don't deserve to be forgiven this time. When he offends me, he brings up the past and says I have no right to be upset.*

I've been so emotionally drained! I don't know if I'm the toxic one causing problems or if he's too sensitive. I've lost the ability to think straight, and I don't know what's right or wrong. I feel terribly guilty for hurting him! I'm a mess right now. It's so complicated with him all the time. I don't know what to do.

You aren't the toxic one and your boyfriend isn't sensitive—*he's* toxic, manipulative, and demeaning.

You must face reality, but *he* doesn't have to? Who demands of someone they love to demean themselves? Is that the reality of loving someone? I talk in a part of my last book, *Things I Wish My Father Had Told Me*, about how relationships don't follow the law of addition—instead, they follow the law of multiplication. In other words, healthy relationships don't consist of half a person meeting their other half to make a loving whole (addition, or ½ + ½ = 1); rather, they consist of a whole person meeting another whole person to form a loving whole (multiplication, or 1 x 1 = 1). Further, I state that, since relationships follow the law of multiplication, a half person forming a relationship with another half person (and we're talking about emotionally incomplete people) ends up leaving each person less emotionally whole than when they entered the relationship (½ x ½ = ¼). In the book, I talk about how both halves are reaching, grasping, trying desperately to be whole through someone else, resulting in no one being satisfied; in fact, both parties are less whole than before the relationship.

Another way this lack of love manifests itself is through emotional abuse, manipulation, double standards, seeking revenge, and leaving the person you "love" feeling "less than." Does love build up, or does it tear down? Does love forgive, or does it resent? Is love judgmental, or is it merciful? Mark Twain said that "forgiveness is the fragrance that the violet sheds on the heel that has crushed it." *This* is love—to leave the fragrance of beauty when hurt, not the fragrance of belittling. The fragrance of concord, not the fragrance of condescension. The fragrance of mercy, not the fragrance of misery.

May I gently suggest that you know this isn't love? If he began the relationship acting the way he does now, would there be a relationship? A good test for whether to be in a relationship with someone, no matter how long you've been in that relationship, is to ask yourself this question: **if s/he acted on our first date the way they act today, would I go on a second date?**

If he told you that you must kneel and lick his feet on your first date, would you have gone on a second date?

If he offended you on your first date like he does today, would there have been a second date?

If you felt as emotionally abused on your first date as you feel today, would you have gone on a second date?

If the answer is no to a second date, it should be no to a relationship, no matter how much time you've invested in that relationship. Even if you've spent ten or twenty years in such a relationship, is it worth spending ten or twenty more?

Please walk away from this, and work on the damage this relationship has caused you before you begin another one.

FOUR

Once a cheater, always a cheater?

Do you believe a man will change for the woman that he decides is his forever? Or do you believe if they've cheated on a past partner that they loved, they will do it to you, too?

Do men change for the woman they want?

Let me begin by offering a disclaimer: I in no way and under no circumstance endorse cheating or try to justify it. Once upon a time, I was a cheater, I am no longer a cheater, and I know that the statement "once a cheater, always a cheater" isn't true. Having been a cheater, however, I understand *why* men cheat.

Most men cheat because they lack emotional courage. A lack of emotional courage makes a man who's dissatisfied with the relationship he's in take the easy way out, instead of confronting the issues in the relationship, or breaking off the relationship altogether. A lack of emotional courage makes a man unwilling to invest what he should into his relationship, resorting instead to objectifying women, and how can you fall in romantic love with women's body parts?

If a man has decided that a woman is his "forever," he's not considering her an assortment of body parts assembled together for his pleasure. He sees *her*, the woman inside and beyond her body—her hopes, her dreams, her fears, and her love. He hears *her*; he's not just being attentive in hopes of sex later. If he's really in love—if he has the real thing—he won't settle for a cheap imitation.

If he cheated in the past, he wasn't truly *in* love, even if he thought he was. He may certainly have been in *lust*, or he may have loved, but he wasn't *in* love. He may have *wanted* to be in love, but either he, the woman he was with, or both prevented it from coming to fruition.

Men need to feel safe (just like women), and if a woman belittles him for his feelings, he will suppress them. **A suppressed man *will* cheat.** He should just end the relationship, but for some reason or another, he doesn't. There are children involved. He's insecure and uses cheating to try to feel more secure.

As for my personal experience, my mother encouraged me to cheat from the time I went back to live with her as a pre-teenager. "Make sure you have two or three women," she would tell me, "so that in case one acts up, you have another one to fall back on." I learned, much later in life, that this was an emotionally protective measure she adopted and passed on to me. I did the work necessary to get in touch with and allow my feelings. It was hard, and it took a long time, but I got there.

Feelings are so important for men! Society only allows men two feelings—happiness and anger. But as I said in my book *Things I Wish My Father Had Told Me*, there are no such things as boy emotions and girl emotions—there are only emotions, and the sooner men allow themselves to feel, the sooner they'll fall in love, find their forever, and cease being so emotionally guarded.

Does a man change for the woman he wants? *Absolutely not.* A man changes for two reasons and two reasons only—because he wants to change, and he's ready to change. If he has changed, and is truly ready to commit to you, he'll commit to you.

FIVE

I can only get off to the image of him having sex with another woman.

D uring my alone time, I can only get off if I picture my partner
*having sex with another woman. Sometimes it's a woman I've
seen him checking out, or a coworker he's close to.*

*I would be destroyed if he cheated on me. After I finish, I get this
post-nut clarity and feel super depressed and paranoid about him cheating on me. I don't think this is normal at all and I don't know why I do
it.*

I'll begin by stating some things that may be hard to hear, but I only
ask that you give them some thought.

You feel badly about yourself, and you believe that you aren't good
enough for him. You want to imagine him getting off by having sex
with you, but can't believe he would, or does. Having sex with him is
something you enjoy, but you don't believe it's something he enjoys

as much as you do, so you imagine him having sex with someone you think he'd rather have sex with. You're turned on by your partner enjoying sex, but you're unable to imagine that he enjoys it with you, so it's the only image where you can see him enjoying himself.

You lack self-confidence and have convinced yourself that there's no way your partner can find you attractive. You see him looking at other women, begin comparing yourself to them, and find yourself lacking. Honestly, he should have more respect for you and your relationship than to do that. Let him know that whenever he looks at other women, whether in person or on websites, it makes you feel unwanted, unlovable, unworthy, and unattractive. If he loves you, he'll want to know what he can do to help you feel beautiful.

Instead of telling you to think positively about yourself or the situation or battle your negative thoughts about it, I'll advise you to focus on a different kind of bad, since it's much easier to shift the thinking from an unproductive bad to a productive bad than from an unproductive bad to excessively optimistic.

Your mind is trying to get you to plan for the possible tragedy of being cheated on by your partner, or even losing him, but you've turned this into self-indictment. Rather than do this, trust the process that'll allow you to survive what would, in your own words, destroy you.

Is there a productive bad? Absolutely, and it's called **premeditatio malorum—the premeditation of evils or adversity**. It's negative visualization—the exercise of imagining worst-case scenarios. It helps you prepare for life's inevitable setbacks.

In Letter 76 of the work penned under the translated title, "The Moral Letters to Lucilius," Seneca said, "Today it is you who threaten me with these terrors; but I have always threatened myself with them and have prepared myself as a man to meet man's destiny. If an evil has been pondered beforehand, the blow is gentle when it comes. To the fool, however, and to him who trusts in fortune, each event as it arrives 'comes in a new and sudden form,' and a large part of evil, to the inexperienced, consists of its novelty. This is proved by the fact that men endure with greater courage, when they have once become accustomed to them, the things which they had at first regarded as hardships. Hence, the wise man accustoms himself to coming trouble, lightening by long reflection the evils which others lighten by long endurance."

If you try to combat your negative thoughts by trying to force yourself to think positively about the relationship, you'll find that negative thoughts still thrust themselves into your mind. They're not your enemy; in fact, they're trying to help you survive by coming up with ways to deal with it before the problems happen. Rather than fight this, imagine the worst-case scenario, and ask yourself what would happen to you if what you feared most came to pass. Would you die? Would you be destroyed? Would life be over? Would you be sad? Would you survive? How would you survive? (Actually, ask yourself this last question and sit with it until you have multiple answers.)

Mindfully expecting the worst things doesn't make them happen or keep them from happening, but prepares you for them, and makes you more able to live with the consequences of negative outcomes. They allow you to plan and prepare for life's setbacks, instead of being shocked by them, pitying yourself, or asking why they should have happened to you. They also allow you to be grateful for the good that happens and not take the good for granted. Finally, they motivate you to do all in your power to ensure a good outcome, so that if the worst happens, you won't live with the regret of knowing you could or should have done something differently.

After you've prepared yourself for the worst, practice gratitude for the present. What's good about this moment? What's good about *you* right now? What's beautiful about you? For what are you grateful? What good things can you say about yourself? What good things can you say about your body? Your mind? Your heart? Be grateful for whatever you can while working on those things you'd like to improve, and you'll slowly become more satisfied with your life as it is.

Six

My boyfriend refuses to reassure me.

I, a 21-year-old woman, have been dating my 20-year-old boyfriend on and off for four years. We've been through a lot, including him cheating on me. I decided to forgive him and try to move past that; however, sometimes I still worry that he might cheat on me again. I communicate this to him, and he makes me out to be a crazy, insecure person who is needy and a bother.

Yesterday, he just blatantly ignored me and hung up when I was talking to him about it. I sent him a message after that telling him that my emotional needs aren't being met, laid out my boundary, and told him to let me know if that's something we could work on together. I told him that ignoring me makes me feel like he's doing something he's lying about, even if he did provide me reassurance. This was last night, and he read the message and never replied.

I don't want to break up. I want to work on this, but it seems like he couldn't care less. The icing on the cake is that we're currently waiting *to see if I'm pregnant because of a slip up last week, so it's making me worried about what the future may hold if this continues.*

Is there anything I can do at this point to reach him?

I'm interested in knowing why this relationship has been "on and off" for four years. Whatever the reason, there's no reason to believe it won't continue to be on and off, since there has been no demonstrated commitment to making it work by either of you. You were 17 and he was 16 when you began dating. Rarely does a 16-year-old male date with the idea of a lifetime commitment. At 16 and 17 years old, the driving force of a relationship is more likely hormones than romance, especially for a guy.

It seems like you've tried to make him take your relationship more seriously than he does. If you're on and off, he knows he can walk away any time he wants, and can come back whenever he wants, since that's what has happened for the last four years.

Regarding your boundary, it's a wonderful thing to have; however, if you don't enforce the boundary, it's useless. It's not enough to say, "This is my boundary." It has to include consequences if the boundary is crossed. However, when you say, "If you don't meet my emotional needs, I will *x*," and you don't *x* when your emotional needs aren't met, you don't have the boundary. A boundary's not a boundary if it's not enforced.

Since he doesn't want to listen when you express your insecurities, that tells you he's not interested in meeting your emotional needs. The question then changes from "how can I get him to meet my emotional needs?" to "what will *I* do since he shows that he doesn't want (or isn't ready) to meet my emotional needs?" The more you ignore his refusal to acknowledge your boundary, the worse you'll feel about yourself, the less you'll respect yourself, and the harder it'll be for you to do what's best for you.

In other words, **there's nothing you can do to reach him if he's not ready to be reached.** *He* must decide if he wants to do this. You can't decide it *for* him. If he's unwilling (or unable) to do it, *you* must be willing to move on.

Let's suppose you're pregnant, and he decides to do what you've been asking for the sake of the pregnancy. You'll be happy, you'll believe that he's finally the man you've needed him to be, and you'll expect him to embrace his newfound maturity in a positive and lasting way. The truth is, though, if he were to change solely because you're pregnant, it won't be a lasting change.

No matter the outcome of a pregnancy, it affects women in ways that are often lost on men, especially young men. Women are forced to face the consequences of a pregnancy in ways that men aren't. Those consequences include emotionally maturing ones. Pregnancy alone won't make a man mature if he doesn't wish and work for it for himself.

The best thing you can do for your own emotional peace, and to prepare to learn to love, is to be true to yourself. Don't lie to yourself. Create boundaries and respect yourself enough to act like you're worth maintaining those boundaries, including doing exactly what you said you'd do if those boundaries are violated—the first time they're violated.

SEVEN

My girlfriend is the most wholesome, beautiful, and kind person I know, and I'm thinking about leaving her.

I have been in a committed relationship with my girlfriend for four years. She's not perfect, but she is incredibly wholesome, funny, pretty, kind, etc. The problem is that over the past months I've been thinking about other women, not just from time to time, but daily. It's gotten really exhausting, because in what should be happy moments I share with my girlfriend, I just feel guilty.

On top of this, six months ago one of my past sexual encounters texted me out of the blue wanting to hook up, and I felt somewhat excited.

I don't know how to proceed from here. I have not cheated on her and will not do that, but I feel like I must tell her about my thoughts. I've been holding myself back from doing that because it might ruin the relationship forever. This is especially hard when I see how happy she is

*and how her eyes sparkle when she looks at me. I feel like I can't be the
one to make her happy and I feel horrible when I'm thinking about these
other women.*

I appreciate any advice.

Let me begin by telling you that what you're experiencing is per-
fectly normal and doesn't mean that you don't love your girlfriend.
Yes, it would be incredibly painful for your girlfriend to hear that
you've been constantly thinking about other women, so you spare her
that pain and bear the burden of your own guilt, but commitment
is stronger than feelings, and they're not the same thing. Telling her
that you've been thinking about other women would be the emotional
equivalent of throwing a hand grenade into the relationship. It won't
make your guilt go away, and instead of one person being distressed,
two people will be devastated. In fact, telling her would be more
self-serving than considerate—you may temporarily feel better about
sharing your secret, but she will be left dealing with this emotional
bombshell for (perhaps) the rest of her life.

But which is more likely—a commitment to fidelity, or never to be
tempted to infidelity? Temptation is part of the human condition, and
it's unrealistic to expect yourself to never be tempted. It's not important that you're tempted (in fact, it's natural)—what's important is
how you handle the temptation.

You create your own guilt by holding yourself to an unrealistic standard. By telling yourself, "I must not be tempted by other women", "Being tempted means I'm not committed to my relationship", "Being tempted must mean that I'm not happy with this
woman", and/or "If I were a better man, I would appreciate who I
have, instead of being tempted by who I don't have", you rob yourself
of the joy you could experience with the woman you love, you produce

your own misery, and you descend into a downward spiral that causes you more and more hopelessness, frustration, despair, and a sense of failure.

At the same time, you struggle with two opposing thoughts: 'I can't be the one to make her happy', and 'I can't tell her because it might ruin our relationship forever'. If you don't believe you can make her happy, it's best to break off the relationship so she can find someone who will, but that would mean the end of the relationship, which you don't seem to want. If the only reason you believe you can't make her happy is because you have these thoughts, that's obviously not true and is an irrational thought. The reality is that you *do* make her happy and her eyes sparkle whenever she looks at you *despite* your thoughts.

Stop telling yourself you must never be tempted by other women, and that doing so makes you a bad man. It's a futile endeavor. Rather, continue doing the greatest thing you can do by repeating, as you have said, that you will not cheat on her. It takes much more strength, courage, character, and humanity to refuse to yield to temptation than it does to deny that temptation is a human experience. Refusing to follow an internal feeling of temptation with any external pursuit is the noblest way you can deal with temptation.

EIGHT

How can I help my girlfriend feel sexy?

*W*e both let ourselves go a bit during COVID, but in the last year we have started eating a lot healthier and have both made some great improvements in our lives. I'm very proud of both of us.

However, my girlfriend is hard on herself, and I think she has a hard time with her body image, no matter where she is on her health journey.

I worked out a lot when I was younger, so it was easy for me to get back into the swing of things. This is the first time in her life she has become more active, so I think she is comparing herself to me and finds it hard.

I just want to help her feel good about herself and all the progress she has made, but I'm not sure of the best way to do that.

Please help me with some suggestions of activities or conversations that might help to boost her self-confidence.

As a man, you live in a different headspace than a woman. For men, societal pressures on us tends to be on our ability to provide, to handle repairs, to be strong, and to protect. For women, their societal pressures tend to be on their ability to look "pretty" (with the accompanying need to count calories, hate their cellulite, and otherwise be physically perfect), have manners, act properly, and always have their lives together.

As a result of accepting and agreeing with certain societal messages, your girlfriend is hard on herself—in fact, she was that way before she met you. She has spent years being self-critical, that type of thinking has become a habit for her, and habits of the mind are extremely difficult to change. As I'm sure you know, until she believes good things about herself, she will remain locked in her self-defeating thoughts. Does that mean that you have no positive influence on this? No, it doesn't, but understand that it'll be like eating an elephant one bite at a time. It can become frustrating when you try to reassure over and over yet see that so much of the elephant is still left.

Though you can't feel good for her progress *for* her, you can tell her, again and again, that you notice her progress and are proud *of* her. You can't *make* her feel sexy, but you can tell her, over and over, how sexy she is, as well as treat her as though she's the most desirable woman in the world to you.

It may feel like it's having little to no effect, but it *is* meaningful for her. **You're a lone voice countering years of negative messages from many voices, including hers.** It may feel daunting, but she will appreciate your lone, positive voice while she works to discover her own.

Tell her you love her and tell her how much in love with her you are. Tell her how beautiful she is. Tell her what she means to you. Spend quality time with her, treating her like the queen she is. Listen to her from the depths of your heart—empathetically, and not just to reply. Don't treat her like there's something wrong with her for seeing herself in a way other than the way you see her, but just continue to reinforce how you see her. Don't tell her she's wrong for seeing herself the way she does; just continue to express what you think and how you feel about her.

Hold her hand, cuddle with her, and give her hugs and kisses often. Surprise her with a romantic evening out or a special dinner at home. Set the mood with candlelight, soft music, and a delicious meal. If she's comfortable with it, buy her sexy lingerie, making sure that you choose something that fits her style and personality. Pay attention to her needs and desires, both in and out of the bedroom. Listen to her when she talks and be responsive to her needs and wishes.

You'll just have to believe that you're chipping away at her negative self-view, because the effects may be too small to notice for quite some time. Have faith—each encouraging thing you say plants another seed of self-love in her, and though it may take many years to produce results, the moments it takes to get there are as necessary as the moments you notice the first bud, the first leaf, and the first fruit. You will help her slowly and meticulously learn to love and cherish herself.

NINE

My boyfriend makes rude comments about my appearance, and I want to break up with him.

M y boyfriend and I started dating a year ago with a 2-month break in the middle. He's said things to me such as, "You need to take a pregnancy test" (after looking up and down my naked body), "your face looks dirty" (I have acne), and "my teeth are straighter than yours."

I know he's said other, smaller things, but the point is that I can't help but let this get to me. He made the teeth comment today and I snapped a bit. He played it off as a joke and said I'm being sensitive because it came after we were telling each other we have bad morning breath. I just think there's a difference between telling your partner their breath stinks and saying their teeth are more crooked than yours.

Is it dramatic to feel like I want to break up with him? He knows how I feel and hasn't even said he's sorry.

People who are critical of others are, as a rule, even more critical of themselves.

Both of you are hurt because of the comments you make to one another, and both of you look to hurt each other because you've been hurt. The fact that you've mentioned only one of the hurtful things you've said to him says to me that there are more hurtful things you say, but you mostly think about (and prefer to share) the hurtful things he says to you.

This habit of criticizing one another is toxic, whether in jest or for real. One never, ever feels better about themselves by putting someone else down, and one never, ever helps another person by non-constructively criticizing them. I don't know anyone who wakes up with fresh morning breath, but what's the point of pointing that out to your partner? What positive thing can be gained from negativity?

The only thing to be gained from constant criticism is emotional damage and an erosion of self-esteem over time. It may also be a sign of being in an abusive relationship, as it's a form of emotional abuse.

Since it's true that being critical means greater self-criticism, the only way to overcome hateful thoughts replaying themselves in your mind is to be less critical of others. As you practice coming from a positive headspace, your self-attitude changes, and you begin to learn to treat yourself in a loving manner. The truth is this: you can't love yourself from a negative headspace, and you can't love others if you don't love yourself. You can need them, you can crave them, you can be desperate for them, you can prefer them to being lonely, but you can't truly love them.

Is it dramatic for you to feel as though you want to break up with him? Absolutely not. But carefully consider the reasons you want to break up with him. Is it because he says negative things to you about you? Is it because he hasn't apologized for saying those negative things? Or is it because you're on a journey to find love, and that begins with preparing to love?

If you loved yourself, you wouldn't allow him to say negative things to you, and you wouldn't say negative things to him. You would think of things that are wonderful about yourself first, then him. It's not to say you'd never have another negative thought about yourself. It's that you would endeavor not to hang out in that negative space, for yourself or for him. And you wouldn't choose someone who wants to hang out in that negative space, toward themselves or toward you.

Should you break up with him? I think so, because neither of you give the other what they need, because neither of you are in the place to do so. Continuing this relationship will only deepen the trench of destruction you create for one another. Separate from him, begin a habit of loving yourself, then don't allow anyone to influence your life that doesn't love you. I'm not talking about the feeling here; I'm talking about the verb. Specifically, saying loving things and doing loving things. Feed yourself a constant diet of love, and you will come to no longer crave the junk food of criticism and non-acceptance.

TEN

I found out my fiancé is an addict. What do I do?

*W*e were together six months and he relapsed, hard. He moved in with me, and he was nodding out for eight days straight, drooling and barely able to talk. He lost his job during this bender. I don't do drugs, so I've never seen anything like this before.

I found out I'm pregnant and told him first thing the next morning before he could take anything. He was genuinely happy, but still got high within two hours of finding out. I have a 4-year-old, so he was kicked out of my house on the eighth day of his bender. I tried taking him to rehab, but he started walking the streets downtown and ended up in the ICU the next day.

It's been four weeks now (two hospital visits later), and he was still lying and getting high until he admitted himself to rehab yesterday. He's been to rehab about five times and has had this problem for 10 years. I understand it's an illness, as the brain of an addict is chemically *hijacked into believing they need substances to survive, but I can't be with someone who's killing themselves.*

I've done everything to help him, and I understand that it doesn't make a difference. I have no family and won't have any support for myself, my 4-year-old, and my new child. An abortion is something I don't think I can do. What do I do?

To begin with, let's talk about something you may be experiencing—something called a "savior complex." Someone suffering from a savior complex feels the need to save or fix others, often sacrificing themselves and their own needs to do so. They may only feel good about themselves when they're trying to save others. They are attracted to vulnerable, needy people—people who seem to need to be rescued. They often believe they're responsible for rescuing others from themselves. This complex often develops in people who've experienced a lot of pain and suffering. They're drawn to troubled people and want to take away their pain and suffering, because they're acutely aware how pain and suffering feels. They may sacrifice their own needs to insist on helping people who don't want help. They may also need to have troubled people in their lives to focus on helping *them* so that they can avoid facing their own problems, like past trauma and present difficulties. It can make the "savior" feel validated, powerful, and important. It's a trait of codependency.

Another trait of codependency is the tendency to stay in unhealthy, one-sided relationships. It sounds like you're considering remaining in this relationship, though it provides you with no benefits. You may think that you can rehabilitate him into a person who will supply support for you and your children, but none of us have the power to make anyone anything we'd like, even if it makes them better. It's healthier to accept his decision to continue using, let go of the fantasy that you can turn him into someone he's not ready to be, and leave the relationship. Believe me, there are worse things than not being in a romantic relationship.

If you want to preserve your happiness, if you want to heal, if you want to live a less stressful life, walk away. It's not your job to change him, and even if it were, he's not ready to change, so you can't. That is one of the reasons for the Serenity Prayer, said by addicts everywhere: "God, grant me the serenity to accept the things I cannot change, the courage to change the things I can, and the wisdom to know the difference." People can become as addicted to other people as they can to drugs.

Respect yourself enough to set limits on which behaviors you'll allow from a partner and stick with those boundaries. If you don't love *yourself* enough to set boundaries, do it for your children. Remember that **you're teaching your children how a partner should treat them by what you allow and disallow in the way a partner treats you.** If you don't want someone to treat your children a certain way, you can't allow them to see you being treated that way. These patterns typically happen generationally, and you must be the person to say "no more" so the patterns don't pass down to your children. It's better to walk away than pass down codependency to your children by staying.

ELEVEN

Should I tell my ex's new fiancé about what happened between us?

I dated my ex for 4+ years (from 2016-2020). This woman birthed my first child, and we were slated to get married, but things didn't end up working out. Fast forward to October 2021—she begins seeing someone else. Three months into their dating, she came over to pick up our daughter, but ended up staying for hours. We hung out, played with our daughter for a while, and then both laid in bed together catching up. One thing led to another, and we were back at it with our old ways. We didn't go all the way, as our daughter was present, but our hands were in places they shouldn't have been when dating someone else. We went our separate ways, and she texted me, begging me not to tell her boyfriend, as she didn't want to lose him.

Fast forward to August 2022, and they're engaged. When discussing childcare and schooling location, the conversation shifted to talking about their engagement. I congratulated her and asked if she was going *to come clean with him, seeing as they were going to be married soon. She turned it back on me, saying I was threatening their relationship because I couldn't get over myself. Clearly, by her reaction, I learned that not only had she not told him, but she had no intention of doing so.*

With all that being said, do I take it upon myself to tell him, so he knows the truth before he goes through with the marriage?

I don't have any intention of being with her again, as I've come to terms with how toxic we were to each other. I don't particularly care for her fiancé, but I know he makes her happy and is good for her. I can't help but feel bad that she's actively hiding this from him.

If you have no intention of being with your ex again, and your ex has shown no further signs that she wants to be with you, the answer's different than if she was still cheating on her fiancé with you.

If you and she felt irresistibly drawn to one another, and neither of you wanted a relationship between the two of you to end, her fiancé would need to know before the marriage ceremony—in fact, as soon as possible. It would be unfair for him to enter a relationship that was a lie, and it would be unfair for the two of you to love one another that way and not be able to proclaim it to the world.

However, ask yourself this question: if neither of you have any intention of being together again, what's gained by you telling her fiancé? I don't wish to sound insensitive, but **their relationship isn't your business, and it's not your job to supervise it.** It's her job and hers alone to tell her fiancé about the indiscretion, and if she chooses not to do it, it's not your job to do it for her.

The more important question to ask yourself is this—why did *you* do it? You knew you had no intention of pursuing a relationship with her, yet you showed a willingness to sleep with her, and may have done so if your daughter wasn't there. What made you want to have sex with someone you've described as part of a toxic relationship? Why were you drawn to her?

You see, you may ask why she did it when she was dating someone else, but only she can answer that question, so only she should ask it. You can only answer the question of why *you* did it. She can't. Were you feeling a moment of weakness? Did talking about old times stir up emotions in you that you had suppressed? Did you just want to get laid, even though you're no good for each other?

In other words, don't put your energy into what you can't control (your ex and her fiancé); put your energy into the only thing you can control (yourself). Are you ready to love again? Is there still some unfinished business between you and your ex that you need to resolve? Is there a part of you that's still hanging on to her, and if so, why?

Think about it.

TWELVE

How do you let go of someone who doesn't care about you the way you care about them?

*F*or the last two years, I've made life decisions based on a guy I really like. He doesn't like me as more than a friend (trust me, he and I have had this conversation). I care about him a lot and enjoy hanging out with and talking to him. He doesn't open up to people easily, and he considers me a friend and likes hanging out, but I can tell his friendship has a deeper value for me than it does for him. He'll be active [on his phone], but clearly ignores my messages for a couple of hours before responding, etc.

My biggest regret is that I recently told him how I liked him as more than a friend, and since then, he's opened up to me less and less. I'm glad we're on the same page and I've been truthful, but me telling him led to nothing, and I feel I've put distance between us.

It hurts me deeply knowing this, but I keep him in my life, and go to great lengths to do so, because I like being around him. How do I move on and realize I need to decrease how much priority I give to him?

You hope to change his mind and haven't fully accepted that you won't. You hope he'll wake up and finally realize what a good woman you are. You fantasize about the day that happens. If you hold on to that fantasy, though, you won't accept the reality, which is that he doesn't want the relationship with you that you want with him.

You go to great lengths to keep him in your life because you think that, someday, he'll realize what he has in you, and you want to be there when that moment finally hits him.

The fact is, you're *not* on the same page but the fact that you think you will be says a lot about how little you really see the reality of your relationship, and how much of it is based in fantasy.

There's nothing wrong with him letting you know he doesn't feel about you the way you feel about him, but to keep him close with wishful thinking only hurts you and your future. Have you accepted his response, or do you secretly hope to change his mind with time and effort? If you value the friendship, you must be willing to let go of the fantasy that it will be more.

You have said that you go to great lengths to keep him in your life because you like being around him. Have you taken any time to consider how he feels about this? In other words, don't only think about what you want—think about what he wants as well, and ask yourself if you're being fair to him by hanging on because of how it feels for you.

Don't let what you want with him consume the attention and energy you can give to other relationships which can bring you joy and fulfillment. Even if he felt the way you do, no one person should bear the sole responsibility for influencing your happiness.

Do you have anyone to talk to about how you feel, who can help you process your emotions? If you don't, you may consider seeing a therapist to help you deal with your feelings.

If you believe that you can hang on to him until he finally gets it, ask yourself this question: **how long will you wait until you're cared for the way you deserve to be?** Is it when someone finally gets their stuff together and realizes you're worth it, or is it right now?

Love yourself enough to prioritize your needs over your fantasies. When you love yourself this way, you're able to love him enough to let him go to pursue his happiness, and you're happy for him finding his own bliss, as you find yours.

THIRTEEN

I don't know how to help my suicidal wife anymore.

*M*y wife and I have been married for two years and together for five. At first, I didn't know how bad her mental health was, but throughout the years it has gotten worse, to the point where she wants to kill herself on almost a daily basis.

If she has a bad day, she wants to kill herself, but if she has a good day, all is right with the world. It could even be something small, like something at her job, and she just wants to end it all, or if I screw up anything, it's a wrap. Or even if her family is having a bad day and they're kind of annoyed, it sets her off.

I'm not trying to speak ill of her. I love her with all my heart, but I just don't know how to help her anymore. She won't seek professional help, and as hard as I try, I can't do anything that helps. I read books about depression and how to help suicidal people. I try to talk to her about it and listen to her, but she wants to be closed off. She cried so badly a few days ago that her eyes were bloodshot, and she threw up everywhere.

I hate myself for not being able to help her better. I feel like the worst husband ever. I need help on what to do because I don't want to lose her, but my mental health is now starting to take a bad turn.

You speak beautifully of your wife, despite your obvious pain. The fact that you want her suffering to end speaks of your love, but the fact that you take responsibility for ending her suffering, especially when she hasn't, is debilitating and self-damaging. Who in this world do you have the power to change? Yourself. Who in this world don't you have the power to change? Anyone else.

The reason your "mental health is starting to take a really bad turn" is because you tell yourself that you *should* be able to help her. That if you could just find the right things to say or do, she'd be better, and the fact that she's not better is because of some sort of defect on your part. That if you were a better husband, she'd be a healed wife. That somehow, it's your fault she's not better.

The things we tell ourselves can make us either bitter or better. They can either make us frustrated or fulfilled. They can either transform us, or they can torture us. The fact is this: there are only two people who can change the things your wife is going through—your wife, and a therapist she allows to help her. She must be ready for help and seek it for herself, and you shouldn't blame yourself for her behavior. Even if you screw up, *she's* responsible for her reaction to it, not you. You're only responsible for the screw up.

Tell yourself that you're responsible for your own behaviors, and she's responsible for hers. Stop accepting responsibility for how she behaves and thinking that you can do anything about it if she's not ready to stop behaving that way. **Be there for her, but don't be responsible for her.** Support her seeking help, but don't support her (or anyone else, including yourself) blaming you for her behaviors. You don't take the credit when she responds positively to having a good day—don't take the blame when she responds negatively to having a bad day. And never, ever hate yourself for someone else's behaviors. They're either their choice or they're beyond their control and they need medical intervention, but either way they're not your fault.

Lastly, I recommend you seek a support group such as the Facebook group Speaking of Suicide, or other online platforms such as Alliance of Hope, Suicide Awareness Voices of Education, The Compassionate Friends, or Crisis Connections to help you deal with your feelings. I truly wish you the best.

FOURTEEN

I need advice on how to stop lashing out at my boyfriend.

*M*y boyfriend and I have been dating for over a year. This has been the best relationship I've ever been in. He's kind, thoughtful, patient, and overall, a good man. He's great at communicating and listening if I have any issues to bring up.

I do need advice, though. We're currently doing long distance. I've noticed that I've been very snappy with him lately. If there's an issue, I bring it up right away, but tend to argue with him more than necessary. It's like I can't stop myself, and then I immediately regret it afterwards.

I haven't always been like this. It's only started within the last month or two. He's communicated to me that it's been hurting him a lot, and he tends to carry these arguments with him. He feels he's being criticized all the time and never appreciated.

I do love him and don't want to continue these toxic behaviors. I personally think it's a product of my environment—I've been super stressed

lately. I guess I'm asking this: how do you effectively communicate with
your partner without making them feel like you're picking them apart?

I don't know your situation, but I'll offer some suggestions that
may be helpful.

When you feel yourself getting angry or frustrated, try taking a
pause and a few deep breaths. This'll help you regain control of your
emotions and prevent these impulsive reactions.

What triggers you to respond this way? You've mentioned that your
reaction is excessive—what do your issues with him remind you of?
Understanding your triggers can help you by separating what others
have done in the past from what he does now, and dealing with those
issues that trigger you so that you don't take them out on him.

Are you holding onto resentment for something from your past?
Does anything about this relationship irritate you because it reminds
you of something someone did before, and do you find yourself overreacting because of it? If this is the case, it's helpful to remind yourself
that "this is the been the best relationship [you've] ever been in", that
this is a new day, not the past, and that you need to forgive whatever
has happened in the past, not because that person or those persons
deserve forgiveness, but because you deserve happiness, freedom, and
the chance to move on with a phenomenal guy.

Do you feel hurt because you're having a long-distance relationship,
and find that you're taking that hurt out on him by being angry with
him instead of dealing with it as hurt? As I discuss in my book *Things
I Wish My Father Had Told Me*, **anger is a secondary emotion,
stemming from the primary emotions of hurt, fear, and frustration.** When one feels that expressing any of the primary emotions
would make them feel too vulnerable, one resorts to the secondary
emotion of anger, because it makes one feel less vulnerable and more in

control. It's not a conscious switch to the secondary emotion, though; it's done as a defense mechanism, to keep from showing one's fragility. However, if you can't be vulnerable with the one you love, with whom *can* you be vulnerable? If you're willing to talk about how the loneliness of a long-distance relationship hurts you, makes you fearful, and/or frustrates you to your partner, you don't have to resort to the destruction caused by anger.

Do you believe you don't deserve him? That you're not good enough for him? Do you think he's too good for you? Do you think you may be subconsciously trying to sabotage a relationship you don't believe you deserve? What are the things you tell yourself about your relationship? Do you believe that, if he really knew you, he wouldn't be into you? Do you believe that because you lack the ability to supply the frequency of physical intimacy that would make him want to stay in the relationship, he may be tempted to leave you? If that's a fear for you, it would bring you closer if you expressed that fear to him and allowed him to reassure you, as often as is necessary.

Finally, take care of yourself and your needs. You mentioned feeling super stressed. It sounds like you don't prioritize your own self-care, such as making sure you get enough rest, doing things that bring you joy, and finding ways to de-stress. Once you do these things, you'll be better equipped to deal with relationship challenges without feeling the need to lash out at him.

FIFTEEN

Why is it so easy for my ex to talk to other guys after our breakup, while I feel so stuck?

*W*e broke up about 2-3 months ago. We had been together for about five years. After about a month of our breakup, she started talking to guys and flirting, but not in a serious way.

However, why is it that I can't bring this side of me out anymore? Why is it so easy for her to do this but hard for me? I am still stuck on her and hoping we can get back together soon, but I know deep down this won't happen. It's like I feel stuck, like I'm still loyal to her when I shouldn't be. I've lost all confidence in talking to women, and I can't be as smooth as I once was.

I think you've answered your own question. You're stuck on her, you hope that the two of you can get back together, so you're not motivated to talk to other women, and the thought of talking to other women makes you feel guilty, because you believe you're betraying the opportunity to get back together with her. But you also say that, deep down, you know it won't happen. That knowledge doesn't stop you from putting your entire life on pause, though, hoping for what you know won't come true. She, however, has accepted the breakup.

You're in what's known as cognitive dissonance. You have two thoughts about your relationship with her that are in conflict with each other, mentioned in the previous paragraph, and the resulting discomfort you feel paralyzes you from moving on with your life. Furthermore, you're immobilized because you can't figure out what you did wrong that caused the relationship to fail, so you don't pursue other women because you're no longer sure of yourself.

You're also in cognitive dissonance because you're stuck in the beginning to middle stages of grief regarding the end of the relationship (using the Kübler-Ross model of the five stages of grief). Part of you is in denial, and part of you is bargaining. Denial that the relationship is truly over, even though you say you know you won't get back together and bargaining in the sense of negotiating with the universe (or God, or fate, etc.) to do whatever it takes to rekindle the relationship. Both of these cause you to be stuck in both the past and a falsely imagined future. The last stage of this model is acceptance. When you arrive *there*, you'll be able to let go of what isn't and move closer toward what could be with another woman, and your voice will return.

The fact that your ex has started talking to and flirting with guys so soon after your breakup doesn't necessarily mean that she's moved on, though. Sometimes people engage in these types of behaviors to try to distract themselves from their pain, or just to feel validated by someone else.

The last thing I will say is this: **don't try to be smooth; be real.** Women aren't looking for the smoothest man; they're looking for the most genuine one. Smooth men are for the movies. Being a man in real life is sometimes beautifully awkward, as is being any human.

Sixteen

I'm being blackmailed by my cheating girlfriend.

My dad is serving life in prison for murder. Nobody at school knows except for my girlfriend. I found out that she's sleeping with another guy when he bragged about it.

She said she still loves me and wants me to forgive and stay with her. She even bought me some gifts to try to buy my forgiveness, but I said no. Now she's threatening to tell all our classmates that my dad is a murderer.

I don't want anyone to find out, since I don't know if I'll be able to handle it. What do I do?

The first thing to do is to **be true to yourself, above all else.** If you don't want to be with her, don't. This advice sounds easier to say than to do but think about it. If you agree to stay with her to keep her from telling others about your dad, she knows that she can do whatever she wants, and she'll get away with it because all she has to do is threaten to tell. Where's the quality in that relationship, for you or for her?

If you stay against your wishes, she has a license to disrespect you, your feelings, and your opinions. She can only tell once, but she can disrespect you for the rest of your life. Which is better? Which is worse?

If you wanted to forgive her because you were interested in continuing the relationship, that would be one thing; however, you want to get out of the relationship, and the only thing that's holding you there is the threat, not love. What would be next: would you have to marry her, or she'll tell? How many things will she get you to do against your will?

If you're willing, you can easily take this power away from her and get your life back. How? By telling others about your father yourself. I know you don't want anyone to know, but the fact is that someone already knows, and more people already know than your girlfriend. There's an entire correctional system that knows he's there. There's an entire legal system that knows he's there. Anyone can look him up online and find out he's there, what he's there for, and his sentence. And what he's done to get there is no reflection on you as a person. He's determined his future, and you determine yours. You're you own man. Don't let your girlfriend take that from you.

Even if you tell one other person, you'll remove the power you've given her over you, and the decisions you make for yourself will be yours to make, and not influenced by her manipulation and extortion.

SEVENTEEN

I fell out of love. What do I do?

I have been feeling like I fell out of love with my boyfriend of three years, and I don't know what to do!

I don't have a specific event that caused these feelings to start. At first, it was the little things—less sex, less quality time—and now I realize we don't go on dates, and I don't get cute surprises like I wish for in a relationship. But now I just don't really want to have sex at all.

We have an apartment (I don't know where I'd go if we broke the lease) and a cat together, and I feel tied down, being just 21 years old. Our friend group has merged into one. Our lives have merged into one.

At times, it feels as though the love is still there. Is it just the routine of life that's making me feel this way? Is it just anxiety and depression? I don't know what it is, but I just want to go back to my normal, happy self.

He treats me amazingly, does whatever I ask, and is very selfless. It's super confusing, because sometimes I feel like I want to buy a house with him, have children, and grow old together. But as of late, it's been hard to imagine that life I used to think of so often.

I don't know what to do anymore. If you have any advice, please help me—I'm all ears.

Sometimes, people simply grow apart, or one person evolves in a different way than another. Sometimes, people just need time apart. Sometimes, the puppy love is gone, which typically lasts somewhere between two months and two years. Though the potential for mature love follows, a choice needs to be made. Do I go to the next level of love with this person, or do we break up?

If you've grown apart, it's important to be honest about it. Let him know how you feel. From the way you describe him, he sounds like the kind of person that'll listen. You can discuss together the process of disentangling your lives from each other, realizing that it'll take time.

If, however, you just need time apart, let him know. You can sleep in different rooms and agree to lead separate lives for a while. If you're able to spend a weekend (or weekends) with family, or if he's able to do so, it'll give you time to think about and assess where you are in the relationship.

Another thing that may be happening is that you believe he takes the relationship for granted. You may believe he no longer does the things he used to do because he no longer thinks he must pursue you. That can certainly be the case. Does he love you as deeply as you'd like to be loved? Are there things you wish he'd do that he isn't doing? Are there ways you need him to show you love that he's not?

If you believe that your relationship is salvageable, you and he should sit down and talk about the things you need from the relationship that you haven't been getting (for instance, gifts, quality time, dates), and together decide to make those things a greater priority. **Communicating your needs is essential!** Since he'll do whatever you ask, he'll be happy to oblige you in these things, and if you're also willing to oblige him in meeting his needs in the relationship, you're on your way to mature, long-term love.

EIGHTEEN

How do I deal with divorcing a woman who wants a polyamorous relationship?

I got married three months ago to a lovely lady whom I had dated for three years. Two months into the marriage, she decided she wants polyamory, she has a partner in mind, and she says it's **my** choice to stay by her side at the end of the day. She went on to plan a relationship with this new person, ignoring my saying how uncomfortable I was with it. Only when the other person's partner said no to the polyamorous relationship did my wife finally say that she could just be friends with her.

Fast forward a month and she quit couples counseling—which she said she wanted—and said divorce is the only choice, because she can't be monogamous.

I'm a caring person in general, and her friends have even commented that I'm more like a caregiver to her than a husband. I've done 90% of the cleaning, appointment making, medicine reordering, and cooking in *the last three years. She continually promised she'd do more, help more, and contribute more.*

I guess I'm asking how to manage a divorce and my own emotions through this mess.

She has told you that divorce is the only option and that she can't be monogamous, so you realize that this is the inevitable course you must follow. Since divorce is the death of your marriage, it's as devastating as experiencing the death of a person you loved or about whom you cared deeply. Treating it like a death gives you permission to grieve your loss, deal with your feelings and memories, and finally move on.

As you grieve, ask yourself this question: even though you do love your wife, how much of that 90% of cleaning, appointment making, medicine reordering and cooking have you done in the last three years simply because you didn't want to be alone? My guess is most of it. Why were you okay with being considered as more of a caregiver than a husband? When you consider that you did all of this to keep from feeling lonely, and yet you feel lonely because she no longer wants to be with you, you must conclude that this loneliness was inevitable.

This should lead you to **ask yourself which would be easier—to be lonely with her, or to be lonely without her?** Your life would be much simpler if you were lonely without her than if her presence remained a constant reminder of what you couldn't truly have.

This is how you manage your emotions—you accept the things you can't change. I know it's easier to say this than to do it, but what alternative is there? To refuse to accept what can't be changed? Doing this leads to unnecessary, never-ending, and unrelievable frustration. Accept that she doesn't care how you feel about her introducing another romantic partner into your relationship. Accept that you can't change her feelings, but you can certainly change your marital status.

In the meantime, give yourself the love you wish you had. Treat yourself—take yourself out on dates, travel, explore, discover. The most powerful way to prepare to love another is to relearn to love yourself.

NINETEEN

My sister's wedding was cancelled because of me, and I feel guilty.

*G*rowing up, one of the things my sister and I most excitedly talked about was having a wedding, and we used to dream of ideal destinations.

My sister was scheduled to get married to a sweet boyfriend whom she had dated for four years. Our family agreed to pay for the wedding, while the groom's family would pay for the honeymoon. We were on a tight budget, and she very reluctantly agreed to have the wedding in our hometown instead of Paris after numerous arguments between me, her, and our mother. She also made her friends buy her expensive gifts and wouldn't take homemade or affordable ones.

The night before the wedding, at the rehearsal dinner, things went downhill. She was drinking more wine than usual and complained that her food wasn't extravagant enough. I kept my mouth shut throughout

*most of it, but when she berated the waiter, I couldn't take it anymore
and called her out for her rudeness and selfishness.*

*At this point everyone, including our mother and her fiancé, was
telling her to calm down, but she decided to throw her silverware at me
and yelled that I was banned from her wedding. Our mother apologized
to me for her behavior, but I left anyway.*

*Still, I wanted her and her fiancé to be happy together. That's why I
now feel a lot of guilt after her fiancé apologized for her behavior and
called off the wedding and their relationship (she continued to get drunk
during the rehearsal dinner, and even slapped him in the face when he
tried to calm her down).*

*I feel that, had I not said anything, the wedding would have taken
place. How do I make this all up to them?*

There's nothing to make up to anyone. Rather than having ruined
their wedding, you did him a huge favor!

There is a Latin saying that goes *in vino veritas*—in wine there is
truth. In other words, people under the influence of alcohol are more
likely to give voice to the things that are true about them that they
would otherwise suppress. I'm sure you know your sister well, and
just as you called her on it when she insisted on a marriage in Paris
and having her friends buy her expensive gifts, you also called her
on it when she acted out under the influence. You correctly called
her out on her childish, selfish, and denigrating behavior. If you were
responsible for the ending of her marriage, you were also responsible
for her being reasonable about not having to get married in Paris. Did
you decide she wouldn't get married in Paris, or did she? Since she was
the one who made that decision, she was also the one who chose to
sabotage her relationship by her drunken behavior.

You (and she) did her ex-fiancé a favor by revealing her true nature to him before it became an expensive divorce. As you said, "she continued to get drunk during the rehearsal dinner, and even slapped him in the face when he tried to calm her down". Imagine how that made him feel, especially in front of the group at the dinner. Can you imagine what *his* family was telling him or how *they* felt? Do you think they told him it was a good idea to marry your sister? Did she create feelings of trust or distrust in the future of their relationship by her behavior? It was he who made the decision to call it off, and it wasn't because of you, but solely because of your sister's behavior.

And remember, though she was drunk, she was still responsible for every awful thing she did. We don't excuse someone who kills someone else because they were drunk and got a DUI—why is any other drunken behavior excused?

Please don't think that you have anything to make up to anyone. Everyone in question (you, your sister, her ex-fiancé, and even your mother) is an adult and, as such, is responsible for the decisions they make, as well as the consequences of those decisions. The lesson to learn from this is one I stated in my earlier book, *Things I Wish My Father Had Told Me*—**choose your consequences, and your actions will choose themselves**. In other words, choose (on a macro level, not just in the moment) what you want your life to say, to mean—choose what you want written on your tombstone, or the dash between the year you're born and the year you die to say about you—and your actions will choose themselves.

The best thing that can come from this is that your sister finally realizes the effects of her toxic behaviors and chooses to get help to overcome them. Hopefully, this was her wake-up call.

TWENTY

She told me she cheated, then she told me she lied about cheating. I don't know what to believe or what to do about it.

My girlfriend told me she cheated on me. Around two months later, she apologized while crying, and it seemed like a heart-felt moment. Even though things have been pretty good between us since then and we love each other, I felt like I needed her to know again that **she cheated on me.**

We talked about it again, and it turns out she was lying. She **lied** *about cheating on me. These are just words, though, and I'll never know if anything ever happened or not. She said she lied about cheating the whole time and about the things she did with him because she just wanted more attention from me.*

Now I don't know what to do. If it's true that she never did anything, I don't want to just give her hugs and kisses and be like "wow haha nothing bad ever happened—I love you" because my feelings were real! I cried and I was heartbroken for so long—it hurt for so long—but now you mean it was all a lie? But what if she's lying about it all being a lie?

I hate this with a passion. I don't want her to get away with this so easily—I was truly hurt and yes, I'd be glad if she really didn't do anything—but I just don't know what to do from here.

What I hear you saying is that this really isn't about avenging your feelings—it's about whether you can trust her, or whether you can't.

For two months, you were heartbroken. For two months, you awaited an apology. For two months, you felt like there was a stranger lying next to you, someone you didn't really know after all. For two months, you suffered alone, while she lived clueless to your true feelings. For two months, you accepted responsibility for her cheating, believing that it was because you weren't giving her enough attention, so you were determined to make it right, despite your personal pain.

Then, she apologized and said she never cheated. Why, then, did she cry? Is it because she felt guilty for cheating, or is it because she felt guilty for lying about cheating? It seems like a melodrama written for a desperate daytime soap opera.

Life is meant to be lived simply, but we make it complicated. It's one thing, however, to complicate life yourself, and it's another to be with someone who multiplies that complication for you. Ask yourself this question: do you trust her? Can you trust what she says to you from this point on? You can, of course, let her know that this was her last time violating your trust, and if she does it again, you will leave, or you can simply leave. But if you make that stipulation, you must mean it. If there's a shred of violation, you must leave. Not because you don't want her to get away with behaving like this, but because you need trust in order to fully engage in romantic love. Also, you'll lose respect for yourself (and she'll lose respect for you) if you don't enforce the boundaries you set.

Don't concern yourself with whether she was cheating or lying about cheating. Either way, she violated your trust. If she wanted more attention, all she had to do was ask for it, not resort to a farce. If you want to keep the relationship, check in with her on a regular basis by asking if you're giving her enough attention, or if you aren't, ask what you can do to make things better. And don't be afraid to make *your* needs known, as well, including the need for her to always be truthful with you.

If you want to keep the relationship, be willing to put in the work, but also be willing to walk away if your trust is ever violated again. However, if you believe that you just can't ever trust her again, it's better to walk away sooner than later. The longer you wait for the inevitable, the harder it's going to be.

TWENTY-ONE

I feel guilty for saying what I need.

*S*o my boyfriend and I have been fighting quite often and heavily. *After every fight he says, "This wouldn't have started if you hadn't blah blah blah." I would like to add that it starts when I explain what's bothering me.*

I told him when we argued I need him to work against the issue as a couple and not against me. He promised me he would change, but he hasn't.

I brought up to him that I don't see us working out if he doesn't change, and now he won't talk to me, seems different, and I feel guilty.

When something bothers you in a relationship, you have not only a *right*, but an *obligation* to express it. The relationship won't improve if you aren't able to effectively communicate your needs, or if he's not willing to listen to them.

Whenever a conversation devolves into an argument, though, it has reached the point where nothing constructive will be done. Arguments are an attempt to force another person to hear you against their will—thus an attempt to force you to hear him against yours.

When he says, "This wouldn't have started if you hadn't [begun telling me what's bothering you]," he's saying that you communicating your needs is why he argues with you. He accepts no responsibility for the arguments, and he's trying to bully you into silence through both the arguing and the emotional isolation he's giving you. He's either unwilling or unable to face issues in the relationship. Unwilling because he feels overwhelmed and doesn't want to deal with conflict, or unable because he has had no model for an effective way to deal with conflict, so he doesn't know how to handle it.

You must resist the urge to point fingers, though. It's a natural reaction when you feel backed into a corner and fingers are being pointed at you, but it's counterproductive. If all you're doing is pointing out what you think is wrong with him, and he responds by pointing out what he thinks is wrong with you, nothing good will be accomplished.

His goal in not talking to you and seeming different is to make you feel guilty, so you won't bring up those things that bother you. He's emotionally withholding to sabotage your efforts to deal with the situations in your relationship, and to a degree it's been working. He may or may not have been doing this consciously, but the outcome is the same.

Please allow me to offer a suggestion for the next time you need to discuss what's bothering you. Try your best to use this construct: "When do you x, I feel y." This is instead of "you make me feel y when you do x." And when you say, "I feel y," be careful to ensure y is an actual feeling, not a thought. How can you tell the difference?

If you can replace, "I feel..." with "I think..." and it still makes sense, it's a thought, not a feeling. For instance, you can replace "I feel that you don't listen to me" with "I think that you don't listen to me", and it still makes sense, so it's a thought, not a feeling. However, if you try to replace "I feel sad" with "I think sad", the second statement doesn't make sense, so you're communicating a feeling. Another way to tell is if you follow "I feel" with "that", as in "I feel that..." Anything after the word "that" is going to be a thought, not a feeling, as in "I feel that you don't listen to me."

Make him responsible for his behaviors, but take responsibility for your feelings about those behaviors, because his behaviors are his responsibility, and your feelings are yours. Most importantly, though—never, ever feel guilty for communicating your needs. It's one of the greatest ways that you can show that you've learned to love yourself.

TWENTY-TWO

It took me a year to realize I've been hurt all along about a breakup.

I broke up with someone over a year ago and just now realized, through therapy, that I still love them, and they were the closest I ever got to "the one." But they have moved on, and I was okay about it for so long that I thought I was okay. I didn't expect to be hurt over the breakup a year later.

Breakups are a form of death, and deaths need to be grieved.

The five stages of grief, according to Dr. Elizabeth Kübler-Ross, are denial, anger, bargaining, depression, and acceptance. For over a year, you thought you had reached acceptance, but therapy helped you see that you were depressed about it.

You aren't in denial over the breakup, angry about the breakup, or trying to bargain with your ex regarding terms and conditions required to get back together. You're grieving what could've been—all the things you hoped for and dreamed would be with this person. Allow yourself to sit in that grief for as long as it takes and realize that this grief isn't something you'll feel only once, but as wave after wave of grief washes over you, eventually each wave will be smaller than the last.

The fact that it took therapy for you to get in touch with your feelings means that you found yourself acting in uncharacteristic, inexplicable ways, which was your unconscious mind trying to express its sufferings to your conscious mind, and this motivated you to seek therapy to get at what was going on inside of you. I applaud you for taking this step.

TWENTY-THREE

My girlfriend is trying to force me to get married and gave me an ultimatum.

*M*y girlfriend told me her mom was coming to visit, and that she'll meet me while she was in town. She informed me of this five days before she was set to arrive. Her mom meets and likes me, then my girlfriend said that she's telling the whole family about me and mentioned that I should go visit her family in December.

The next day, her brother mentions to her that we should get engaged in December. She tells me about it and I'm like mm-hmm. She jokingly talks about getting married all the time, so I think nothing of it.

A week goes by, and she mentions a few times that I'd better get her a nice ring and I don't say anything more than mm-hmm, then one day she says I'm dress shopping for December, and that's when I realize she's being serious, and I tell her that we haven't even talked about this, and she agrees that I'm right and she was getting overexcited.

The next day I pick her up, and as we're in the car, she mentions that she just bought a dress for December, and I say you never asked me about any of this and that I have no plans of getting engaged in December. She tells me that she's already told her family she's getting engaged and asks why I'm doing this to her. I tell her she's not being logical; she's only doing this because her family's forcing it on her—after all, I've only known her for one year.

Then she says I need to tell her mom that we're not getting engaged in December, and I tell her I'm not dealing with all that right now, then she just breaks up with me on the spot and walks off.

This all happened over the course of two weeks. I'm in my late 20s and she's in her early 30s. I was open to marriage, but I'm not going to get forced into marrying someone.

Since then, she has sent me more than 50 text messages and called me over 20 times. I haven't answered the phone calls, but she's trying to act like she didn't break up with me and she's apologizing, saying she's in the wrong, but I think it's only because she's trying to do anything to keep me from leaving her.

She told her mom the engagement was off. I told her I'll play whatever role she needs me to play until her mom leaves in a few days, and that we're taking a break after she leaves.

For some reason, she saw you as a person who would give in to pressure, if enough was placed on you. She saw that she couldn't apply an effective amount of pressure on her own, so she recruited her family to help her. When she saw that didn't work, she walked away, hoping that you would be desperate enough to do anything to get her back, to include marrying her. When that didn't work, she ran out of options and decided to try to at least get things back to the way they were.

Marriages that happen because one party wants it and the other party is pressured into it are one of the reasons for the saying, **"Marry in haste, repent in leisure."** Both parties will end up regretting getting married, because it won't fulfill either party's expectations of what a marriage should be.

You said you plan on taking a break from the relationship when her mother leaves, but what do you hope to achieve by doing this? Do you hope she'll realize the harm in her actions, and vow to never do them again? Are you waiting until you believe her when she says she was wrong for what she did, instead of thinking she's just saying it in order to try to keep you from leaving her? Or is this just a less truthful way of quitting the relationship? In other words, if you plan to take a break, it should be with a goal, so that when it's accomplished, the break's over. If you plan to take a break but have no goal for the break, what you're doing is as unfair to her as what she did to you—leaving her hanging on until some nebulous, undescribed, undetermined moment.

Are you punishing her for her behavior? If so, when will the punishment be over? When she's learned her lesson? If so, how will you know when she has? And if punishment is the goal, hasn't her humiliation with her family sufficed?

I recommend that you decide if you still want the relationship, then stay if that's what you choose, or leave, if that's what you choose, but taking a break is a generic term often used for indecisiveness, or a coward's way of leaving a relationship without saying so.

TWENTY-FOUR

How do I break up with my grieving boyfriend?

*M*y boyfriend and I have been together for almost two years. He lost his father about two weeks ago. I've been with him throughout, doing whatever I can to support him. After the funeral, his cousin began living with us.

We have not been intimate since then, and I wasn't rushing him into it. However, his cousin has been hitting on me ever since he came to live with us, and I've obviously been ignoring his advances. The last time he tried it, I told him I would let my boyfriend know, and he said that "it's been a while for you so you should be grateful". I asked him what this meant, and he told me that my boyfriend has been seeing escorts.

While I didn't want to believe this, I did violate my boyfriend's privacy and went through his call history as well as emails (he doesn't have any passwords). I searched for the contact number I found, and it led back to some escort ads in our city.

I want to break up with him, but seeing how he is still mourning his dad and not taking it well and considering that the last time I tried breaking up with him he threatened suicide, I don't know how. How do I break up with him?

Obviously, your decision to break up with him is not a new one, and not one that was decided solely because of the escorts. He's someone you've wanted to break up with, and he selfishly used the threat of suicide to get what he wanted, while not giving the relationship what it needed.

First, **grief is no excuse for bad behavior.** Though a person grieves, they're as responsible for their behavior as someone who drunkenly committed a DUI and injured or killed someone while under the influence. He's responsible for cheating on you, grief or not, and should be held accountable for his bad behavior. You're concerned that he's not taking the passing of his dad well, but he's not concerned that you're not taking his being with escorts well. If you want to break up with him, break up with him.

Second, **you aren't responsible for his decision to commit suicide.** He may blame it on your decision to break up with him, but it's *his* decision to commit suicide, and it will *never* be your fault. Don't stay with him because he threatens to hurt himself if you don't. How is that fair to you? Where's the care for how *you* feel about being in the relationship? Does one-sided happiness equal a relationship? Again, if you want to break up with him, break up with him.

I don't think you're really asking *how* to break up with him, though. I think you're asking how to break up with him while guaranteeing he won't hurt himself, and the answer is there can be no such guarantee. In the end, you must do what's best for you, and if he decides to go through with his threat of suicide, that's his choice, and his choice is something you can do nothing about. Here's where you have control—don't sacrifice your happiness on the altar of his selfishness.

TWENTY-FIVE

I realized my wife has had an emotional affair for the last four years, and I don't know what to do.

*T*he past two weeks have been hell for me.

We've been married for nine years and have two beautiful kids. I caught my wife last week chatting with someone, and when I confronted her, she said it was just a casual talk with a friend for stress relief, and that it started a few months ago.

As I dug up more evidence, she gradually admitted that the affair started four years ago, and now has finally admitted that he was her ex-lover in college. She apologized and said that she would end it for good, and that she's ashamed of herself for having continued it for so long.

But I find myself obsessively rewinding all the things we have done over the last four years. She had the affair throughout almost half of our

married life, through the birth of our second child, and even when I was
hospitalized.

I can't seem to move on and have a gnawing feeling of doubt mixed
with anger, jealousy, and sadness.

I'm pretty sure one of the questions you ask yourself is this: 'If I
hadn't caught her, would she still be in that relationship?' Given the
evidence, the answer is yes.

What's the evidence? You caught her chatting with someone. She
lied about who it was so she could continue the relationship. She
offered no further truth about what was going on until you dug it up.
You had to catch her every step of the way before she would admit
to any of it. She only apologized when she got caught, not when she
should've felt guilty.

It makes sense that you can't move on. All your questions
haven't been answered. Questions such as why did this happen? Has
she carried a flame for him all these years? How far have they gone in
this relationship? Has it only been an emotional affair, or in the four
years it's been going on, have they slept together? How could she stand
to pretend nothing was going on, living in the home with you, sleeping
in the same bed, living side by side every day for the last four years?
How can you know it won't resume, with her being more careful not
to get caught next time?

The doubt, anger, jealousy, and sadness you feel are completely
normal, and need to be addressed, but this is too emotionally charged
a situation to try to work on with just the two of you. The best way
to do this, if you want to save your marriage, is to enter therapy with
your wife.

A therapist will act as an advisor, a listener, a model, an umpire, a
clarifier, and a guide. The process of going through therapy will help

both of you find the things that caused you to arrive where you are in the marriage and will guide you toward where you want the marriage to go. It will be a safe place for both you and your wife to express your innermost thoughts and feelings in a nonjudgmental atmosphere, and gently allow you to examine how certain thoughts and feelings are counterproductive for a successful marriage. Finally, a therapist will give you tools to help overcome the obstacles in your marriage and will help you both through the hard work it will take to bring this marriage back from pain to pleasure, and perhaps even to passion.

TWENTY-SIX

I'm not attracted to my wife anymore.

I need some advice. I'm a 40-year-old man. I've been married to my 49-year-old wife for 15 years, and we have two teenage children. She's a good mom and a decent partner, but I'm not attracted to her anymore, and I feel conflicted about what to do next.

When we met, obviously things were different, but it's changed over the years. She's gained at least 150-200 pounds, and I don't even want to be intimate with her. I'm sure she knows on some level, since we barely have sex anymore, and when we kiss, it's about as passionless as it can be.

I've tried talking to her about it before, taking the angle of "I'm worried about your health"—that didn't work. I've tried cooking healthier and being more active together. It just never sticks, and it seems that if I'm not leading the way, she won't do it. Every time we start to go down the path of being more active or healthier, she turns it into this huge, grand production about how we must overhaul our entire lives *instead of just trying to make small, incremental changes, so it never goes anywhere. Frankly, it's exhausting.*

I'll be the first to admit, I'm not the greatest physical specimen, but I've tried to keep my body in relatively decent shape over the years. I exercise regularly, I try not to eat a lot of garbage food, and I cook healthy meals.

Beyond the physical, I don't know...I just feel distant and unconnected. We still have things in common, but it feels like we're roommates and not spouses. Our interactions are routine and boring. There's just nothing there. I care about her, but I don't think I'm in love with her anymore.

I don't want to spend the next 15 years of my life married to someone whom I'm not attracted to. I'm totally unhappy, and I can feel it building into a crisis. I'm increasingly thinking about divorce, but obviously, I'm worried about the fallout for her and the children. I don't know what to do.

It sounds like your situation overwhelms you. I imagine it's at least as overwhelming for her—probably even more so. What do you do when so many things seem to conspire against you all at once—increased weight, hormonal changes, menopause or pre-menopause, and everything that goes with all that?

It sounds like she really does want the "huge, grand production", and needs your support to make it happen, but it's something you're not willing to do. She obviously doesn't believe she can stick to any diet without it. If other areas of your lives together were more loving, you might be willing to offer the "huge, grand production", so let's focus on those areas.

What about her, other than her physical appearance, did you find attractive enough to marry 15 years ago? What made you feel connected then that doesn't exist now? What did you do that made your interactions interesting and meaningful that you no longer do? Have you sat her down and talked to her about any of your feelings? If not, is it because you believe it would upset her too much to hear you say how you really feel? If you believe it would be too upsetting for you to be honest with her about your feelings, do you think it's better not to talk about them than to contemplate divorce?

Have you decided divorce is the best way to go about this, despite the effects on your wife and children, or are you willing to do what it takes to not only keep the marriage afloat, but to allow it to thrive? If you're willing to choose the second option, I have a few suggestions.

First, I recommend you talk to your wife about how you feel. Though you may be concerned that such a conversation may hurt her feelings, she must already know there is something wrong with your relationship. Talking about it and being honest about your feelings and frustrations will, at a minimum, confirm the things she already suspects, as well as supply an emotional release for you.

Second, both of you may want to further this conversation with a therapist. A therapist will be able to help you both ensure you understand what the other person feels and will allow you to continue the conversation in a non-judgmental and safe environment. Also, a therapist is an amazing umpire who ensures conversations won't get so heated that they become counterproductive.

Third, ask your wife if she's willing to see a medical doctor to help her reach her goals. It may take a team of medical professionals, each focused on a certain aspect of her health, to help her reach her goals—not just weight goals, but hormonal goals, as well. Relief in those areas will cause her to become more receptive to the idea of seeing herself as desirable and sexy, which she doesn't see herself as now. If she doesn't see herself as desirable and sexy, she won't allow herself to believe she's worth your time and attention.

Zig Ziglar says, "You can have everything in life you want, if you will help other people get what they want." Help her achieve happiness in the relationship, and you will achieve happiness in the relationship. Help her feel desirable, and one day you may desire her again. But you must be patient and willing to help and support her life changes with some drastic life changes of your own.

I understand that you must feel it's worth it in order to be motivated to put in the work, and you may not feel it is. If you don't, I wish you well with your next relationship. But remember this: in preparing to love, realize that *all* **love is effort, whether it's loving oneself or someone else.**

TWENTY-SEVEN

I take frequent restroom breaks at work and feel uncomfortable about it.

I've been working for this company for two months. I use the restroom about every 90 minutes, and while no one has even mentioned anything about it, I often get looks every time I excuse myself from my desk. I try to be quick, since I'm extremely sensitive about how often I go. At most, I'm gone for three minutes.

I'm diabetic, which is why I constantly must relieve myself. I don't want them to think I'm going to the bathroom to waste time or that I'm a lousy co-worker. I do need this job, and I enjoy my co-workers. Would it be weird if I shared why I'm always excusing myself?

First, I recommend you don't share why you always excuse yourself from your desk, since it's no one's business (except for your supervisor, and even then, you don't need to be specific; you can just let them know you have a medical condition that makes you need to use the restroom every 90 minutes or so). Furthermore, it's likely that few people, if any, care that you go to the restroom so often.

Second, might I suggest you don't look at anyone for their reaction when you go to the restroom? **The next time you go, just focus on your destination, not the journey.** Because you're so worried about your co-worker's reactions, it's possible that you're reading into their facial expressions and body language things that are simply not there. Since you think, 'they must think badly of me for having to go so often' and 'they must think I'm deliberately wasting company time and using the restroom as an excuse to do so', you can't help but see that in their faces. If we realize how little people think of us, because they're so preoccupied with their own lives (and we're not *that* important to them), we will change our whole perspective about things. Suppose you thought, instead, 'these people have their own lives—mine isn't as important to them as I think'. How might that change the way you see things?

Finally, the journey of preparing to love begins with learning to love oneself. A part of that is allowing your journey to be without self-judgment. You have diabetes. A side effect of it is having to go to the restroom more often than others. Let that be without your judgment, or worry about what others think, since neither will change the reality of the situation. In the spirit of the Serenity Prayer, accept what you can't change, change what you can, and know the difference between what you *can* change and what you can't.

TWENTY-EIGHT

Why would people want to date me when there are other, better suitors?

*T**his thought occurred to me when I noticed an attractive person walking by. I thought it would be nice to get to know that person, but then remembered that there are other people with better looks, income, and personality. And there are times when others ask me out, but I've always wondered whether they only did so because they can't get with other girls out of their league.*

From my past experiences, people would always prefer those with better qualities (e.g., income, looks, and personality) and would jump ship easily if presented with the opportunity. (In the past, I've seen both my male and female friends do this.)

This makes me feel very insecure. I'm scared to get into a new relationship. It always feels like I'm the ship that people get on just because they can't get onto another, better one. What's the point of dating if there's always someone better than you?

There'll always be someone "better" than you in someone else's opinion. Imagine if everyone wondered what the point of dating would be because someone on this planet didn't consider them the "best"—that there's someone else on this earth that's "better". No one would ever date!

But let's start by looking at the things that you say make others better than you—income, looks, and personality.

Is better really defined by income? If that were true, it would mean that the more money you have, the better you are. The better what? Does a larger asset portfolio make a better person? By what standards? Just a passing observation at being human shows that that's the wrong way to think of worth. What makes you any less a human being than anyone else, whatever their income? What is essential for human being-ness? Isn't it simply to be, as in human *be-ing*? That leaves no room for other definitions of worth, such as income. Yet how many people with money think those with less are worth less? Or even worthless? Don't agree with their opinion! Learning to love yourself begins by loving your being-ness, apart from anything else.

Is better really defined by looks? So the more handsome or beautiful one is, the more they're worth? Is beauty the main thing one looks for in a potential partner? We all know people who are beautiful on the outside, but rotten, ugly, and disgusting on the inside. Their personalities wipe away any benefits they may have by being beautiful. And who would you rather be with—someone who's beautiful on the outside, or someone who's beautiful on the inside? (That's not to say that a person can't be beautiful both inside and out.) And even if you find yourself still stuck on someone who left you because they found someone more beautiful than you, realize that no matter how beautiful the new person is, there's someone who's more beautiful than them. Also, even if you were the most outwardly beautiful person in the world today, that could easily disappear by being a victim of an accident or simply by aging. True beauty, which is inner beauty, can never be taken from you, and that's the beauty you should focus on cultivating. Lastly, remember that the saying is true: beauty *is* in the eye of the beholder. Though you may not consider yourself particularly beautiful, believe someone else when they do. In the meantime, love yourself enough to believe you're worth having a wonderful relationship with a devoted partner.

Also, what are the traits of what you'd consider a great personality, and what's stopping you from developing those traits? Is it a traumatic past? Is it because you've been hurt, and that's left you jealous and suspicious? Whatever the reason, and whatever you believe you lack in personality, there are some things that can be changed, while there are others that should be accepted. For instance, if you'd like to be more loving to people, you must do the hard, hard work of forgiving those who have hurt you—not for their sake, but for yours. However, if you're an introvert and you believe being an extrovert is better (neither is *better* than the other), you will continuously deny yourself happiness. It would be much better to, again, accept those aspects of your personality you can't change, while changing those aspects of your personality you can.

Finally, may I suggest that you're treating potential relationships like sour grapes? This analogy comes from one of Aesop's fables, titled The Fox and the Grapes. In the story, the fox is hungry and happens upon a vine full of grapes. Relieved at finding food, he stretches for the grapes to eat them, but they're too high for him to reach. Try as he might, he simply can't touch the grapes. Disgusted by his inability to reach the delectable fruit and unwilling to admit that his efforts have been defeated, he says, "Those grapes are probably sour anyway" as he sulks away.

How does this story apply to you? Rather than admit that you're sabotaging your own efforts at having a relationship, and that you're scared because of your own beliefs about your desirability (instead of actually being undesirable), you call yourself the "ship that people get on just because they can't get onto another, better one"—in other words, you're calling yourself sour grapes. There's enough negativity in this world—please do yourself a favor and don't create your own. **Instead of thinking about why someone wouldn't want you, remind yourself, over and over, why someone *would* want you.** Stop talking yourself out of a chance to love and be loved.

TWENTY-NINE

Do I have self-destructive tendencies?

R *ecently, I've noticed a pattern. I can't tell if it's just because I just can't like people, or if it's just me ruining it for myself.*

Every time I'm interested in a girl I like, I notice that I tend to come to resent her and lose all feelings I used to have. For example, there's a girl I really liked. We were fooling around, and it was nice. I told her when we first started that I really liked her and wanted to date, but she wasn't sure and wanted to be friends with benefits. I didn't mind, and I liked her still the entire time, but we hung out one night and she said, "I don't know if I'm falling for you," and in that moment I lost all feeling and got sad almost, like she had rejected me. I can't tell why.

It seems like when you're interested in a girl and she expresses interest in you, you suddenly lose interest. It could be that, in that moment, you're disappointed in her decision to fall for you—perhaps because you don't feel you deserve such a thing.

You may "lose all feeling" because you spend so much time putting yourself down in your own thoughts that you prefer relationships that don't seem like real ones, so that the minute they seem to become real, you emotionally check out.

The feeling of resentment could be from an expectation of rejection. Do you find yourself spending time thinking of women walking out on you? Do you believe that women, if they really knew you, would want nothing to do with you? Do you feel yourself a nobody, and able to fool women into thinking otherwise, but only for a while? Do you dread that, whenever you're in a relationship, you'll eventually get found out, and being left is inevitable?

I think you got sad because the reality of your self-rejection convinced you of a possible future rejection by another, so the answer is in learning to love yourself. How does that look for you?

Write down the reasons you reject yourself and are otherwise unworthy of a real relationship. Ask yourself how true the things are that you've written down. Now take what's true and split it into two lists. The first list will be those things you've written down that you can do something about. After each thing, write down what you're going to do to change it. Break each thing down into smaller goals. Then go about doing those things.

The second list will be those things you've written down that you can't do anything about. Now comes the harder part—harder than the list you can do something about. Take the time you need to list **why you deserve love, despite those things**. And begin that list by writing why you deserve to love yourself, despite your shortcomings. "Because I want love" won't make you feel you deserve it and saying that you want it won't convince you that you deserve it. *Why* do you deserve it?

You deserve it for the same reason masterpieces do, and you need to do as little to earn the right to be loved as they do. Do the hard work of realizing and accepting the masterpiece you are, and you will understand why you deserve it. And understand this: a masterpiece isn't just a good work of art, or even a great work of art—a masterpiece is a rare, one-of-a-kind work of art. And you are that rare—there's no one like you in all the world.

Most of all, remember that what you lack can be overcome by who you are.

THIRTY

How do you communicate your needs in a relationship?

I'm a man in a beautiful relationship with my girlfriend. Things are good, but as a child, I wasn't allowed to express my needs, and learned not to ask much from anyone, expect anything from anyone, and be self-responsible.

Now that may be useful in life, but not in this relationship. I'm supposed to be able to communicate needs like intimacy, attention, and other things I haven't figured out yet, and now I'm suddenly feeling resentful towards my partner, because I expect her to make me feel a certain way and she doesn't (she has no clue I feel this way so don't blame her), so I guess I'm weak in the communications department.

How do I figure out my needs and communicate them in a healthy way?

That's really an excellent question, and good insight into your lack of self-knowledge. I commend you for your willingness to learn.

First, the fact that you weren't allowed to express your needs, learned not to ask much from others, or expect anything from anyone as a child isn't how life is done in the real world. Learning to be self-responsible is useful, but not if it's at the expense of your ability to express your needs.

Therefore, you need to learn how to figure out your needs, and then you need to learn how to communicate those needs.

In saying that you weren't allowed to express your needs, you've opened the door to answering your first need. That is, even though you weren't allowed to do it as a child, you're no longer a child, and are now able to parent yourself. So find a quiet place, still yourself, and ask yourself this question: **what does the child in you need?** Think about the longing you had, as a child, to express your needs. What is it that you wanted to say? What exactly did you want to ask for? You can now ask yourself for those things that you wanted to ask of others. I would encourage you to write down those needs as you think of them, and to really take some time to do this exercise. You will address many, if not most, of the things you need this way.

Next, ask yourself how many of those things you need are in your power to supply yourself. For instance, you need to feel loved by your partner, right? But before you can accept that love from her, you must love yourself and accept love from yourself. If you don't believe you're worthy of love from yourself, you won't accept love from anyone else, no matter how much love they give you. Do you love yourself, flaws and all? Are you willing to *accept* love from your partner? Even more importantly, since you weren't allowed to communicate your needs as a child, are you willing to be vulnerable enough to communicate them now?

So to communicate your needs in a healthy way, make sure that you continue to not blame her for not meeting your needs. Instead, tell her that you know you've been bad at communicating your needs, let her know that you'd like to get better, ask her to be patient with you while you learn to do so, and then begin, with whatever ability you have, to communicate your needs to her.

Communication is an art that only gets better with practice, so don't feel discouraged if your first attempts don't yield the results you want. Continue working on it, get better at it, encourage her to do the same, and you will see your relationship continue to grow.

THIRTY-ONE

Why is my husband making rude jokes about me in front of his friends?

*W*e've been together over two years, and he acts romantic to me in private. I can think of four or five times when he's embarrassed me in public, and it's getting worse each time. He recently told his friend after drinking that he's only with me for my body and that I'm crazy.

I confronted him about this, and he minimized it and apologized. He says he loves me, but I don't know if he's faking it. He may be in love with being in a relationship, but not with me.

My main concern is that, somehow, the rude jokes mean he's a cheater. Could that be possible, or is that too far in the reach of the imagination?

It's unlikely that the rude jokes alone mean that he's a cheater. Rather, they could mean that he's trying to impress others by acting like he can treat you in a manner less than you deserve, and despite it, you'll stay. In other words, he may be trying to impress others by the hold he has on you.

Why would he do this?

Perhaps it's because of his immaturity. It may be that he's worried about what others think of him (which would speak to his level of maturity), and feels he needs to impress them by acting more casual about his feelings for you because he's afraid of being seen as henpecked or subjugated by you. In other words, he may be afraid of being seen as vulnerable in front of his friends.

How vulnerable is he to you in private? Does he seem afraid to express his emotions? Does he seem to think it unmanly to express his feelings for you?

Are the romantic things he does physical things, or emotional things? Opening a car door, pulling out a chair for you to sit on, or walking nearest the street on the sidewalk are all grand gestures, but require no emotional investment. What has he done to emotionally invest in your relationship, or does he seem capable of doing so? Do you believe he takes you for granted on a day-to-day basis?

Rather than being in love with being in a relationship, he may be afraid to be alone, but also afraid of being seen as vulnerable. This may be a good line of questioning to pursue with him. Does he want to be with you because he loves you, or is he there because he's scared of being alone? I'm sure you don't want to be with someone who's simply with you to avoid loneliness.

He has apologized for his rude remarks—that's good. Now he needs to tell you why he's in the relationship and do so until you believe he wants the relationship with you. And he needs to be unashamed to be seem as being in love with you to his friends.

I recommend you make this a gentle ultimatum.

THIRTY-TWO

Is this cheating?

*M*y husband told me he had to work a little longer than usual but met up with a female coworker at the Dollar General that is close to his work.

His explanation was that he was just trying to talk to her and give her some motivation, but I had already been a little anxious about her before this. She always sends him winky faces and seems a bit flirty to me in their texts. And I've made my being uncomfortable with her messaging him known to him, but he does nothing about it.

I'm just so overwhelmed, and the only reason I even found out this happened and was able to confront him about it is because I saw his location on Google Location. I wasn't even looking for him—I was trying to figure out the name of the gas station I stopped at the day before because of their pricey preauthorization for gas. He said he didn't want to make me mad by telling me, but now I'm looking at him disgustedly for lying about his whereabouts to me.

There's no way he's cheating, right? Or am I just being delusional in wanting to believe him?

There is a real possibility that he *is* cheating—if not physically, then emotionally, or at least allowing for those behaviors that lead to cheating. The fact that he won't acknowledge that he's being flirted with, along with refusing to change his behavior based on your being uncomfortable with it, and lying about his whereabouts, all indicate that he has no intention (at least right now) of giving up this behavior.

He didn't tell you he was meeting this female coworker. If his reason for meeting with her was to offer motivation, why lie about it? Since he knows you're uncomfortable with the messages she sends him, why hasn't he done anything about it?

Of course, you want to believe him. **Who *wants* to think their partner is cheating?** But assume for a moment that he is. What will you do about it, besides mourn?

Will you leave him? Will you give him one more chance? Will you confront him? Will you give him requirements in order for your relationship to continue, such as his being transparent about all smartphone interactions? Will you require him to cut off all communication with this woman? Install a location app on his phone? Will you talk with him about things you both can do to improve the relationship? Will you insist that you both see a marriage therapist?

Carefully consider what you'll do *since* he's cheating (in one form or another, otherwise he wouldn't have to meet in secret), instead of wondering if he is, and do it.

THIRTY-THREE

Found my boyfriend's profile in dating mode on Bumble.

*S*o my boyfriend and I decided to sign up on Bumble BFF to get
friends a few months back (we have a serious shortage of friends, so
we thought it would be a great way to make some friends). My profile
had our pictures together, and it was clearly mentioned that I'm in
a relationship. I never checked his Bumble BFF account to see how his
profile looked, as I trust him.

I made a friend, who's a girl, from the site, we instantly connected,
met at a café, and I deleted my Bumble BFF profile after that. My
boyfriend said that he was unsuccessful in finding anyone and had
removed his profile.

I didn't think much about it after that. Fast forward two months, and
I saw a charge on his Apple ID which said that he had been a Bumble
subscriber for two consecutive months! It was a red flag for me!

I didn't ask him about it because I didn't want him to know I knew.
Instead, I asked one of my friends to sign up on Bumble to see if she could

*find him on it. After hundreds of left swipes, we finally found him! His
profile was in dating mode, he had no mention of being in a relationship,
and he had no pictures of us whatsoever! We've been together for seven
years, and this is utterly heartbreaking.*

*My friend dropped him a message to see if he would reply. He swiped
right on my friend, and my friend dropped him a flirty text, to which he
replied that he was already taken. He ended up telling me that there was
this girl who was trying to flirt with him on Bumble, which he reinstalled
yesterday (which was obviously a lie, since he never deleted it in the first
place), and he wondered why people don't want to just be friends online.*

*We didn't talk about it after that. I don't know what to make of all
of this. It's like I'm caught in the middle of half lies.*

It's possible that your boyfriend isn't fully committed to your relationship but is keeping his options open. Does he act like the two
of you are together when you're in public, or does he hesitate to give
a public display of his commitment to you? If the two of you don't
typically have much public interaction (hence the need for Bumble
BFF), make a point of scheduling something you must do in public
and see how he responds to you when you're there.

On the other hand, he may have simply been looking for validation,
which is why he didn't follow up on your friend's flirty comments. Do
you think that's the case? When's the last time you both complimented
each other, or made one another feel special? This is no way excuses
his lies, but it can give you a basis for improving your relationship, if
that's what you choose to do.

However, you may be struggling with that very thing. Do you *want*
to continue the relationship, knowing that he hid his activities from
you and lied about them (and lied about his relationship status)?
You mentioned that you've been together for seven years, and you're

utterly heartbroken by his behavior. **Don't let the thing known as "sunk cost fallacy" determine whether you should stay in the relationship.**

Sunk cost fallacy, in your case, is believing that, since you've invested seven years into the relationship, it would be a waste of those seven years to leave it, when it may be more beneficial for you to leave it and start over with someone else (hence the reason why the sunk cost is a fallacy). Ask yourself this question: can you live seven more years the way your last seven years have gone with him? Or even this question: given what you've learned about him and the things he's done over the last seven years, would you start a relationship with him today if you already knew those things? If the answer is yes to either of these questions, talk with him about what you've discovered, and work on making the relationship honest. But if the answer is no to either of these questions, it's best to cut your losses and move on.

If, on the other hand, he was just looking for validation, it's an easy fix (if you choose to do so). You can give him what he needs (validation) while telling him what you need (honesty).

THIRTY-FOUR

Fiancé said he regrets the night he met me.

*I*confronted my fiancé about why he liked so many of his female friends' pictures (especially a girl I've caught him following online a few times, even though they haven't spoken in over a year), and he told me to "go fly a kite". He then said to me that his biggest mistake was meeting me for coffee back in 2019, which is the night we met.

He has said some hurtful things to me, like "who would want to bring someone like you around?" "No one would be proud to show you off," "if I knew you then like I know you now, I never would've been with you," and so much more. I feel unappreciated, unloved, disrespected, and I don't believe I deserve to be treated this way.

We have an eight-month-old son together, and I'm just at a loss. I don't think someone who can talk to me like this, let alone walk away from me when I'm talking to him and turn the lights off in the room I'm in, loves me. I think he went too far this time, and it hit a final nerve with disrespecting me and not treating me like a fiancé.

He's telling you everything you need to know regarding how he feels about the relationship. He believes that his biggest mistake was meeting you. He doesn't want to bring you around others. He doesn't want to introduce you as his fiancée. He doesn't want to show you off. He regrets being with you. All that's left is for you to believe him, and believe him you must, for the sake of your emotional and mental health.

He doesn't respect you, and he knows that you don't respect yourself, which is why he continues to say the things to you that he does. If you respected yourself, you wouldn't allow yourself to go on feeling unappreciated, unloved, and disrespected. You wouldn't let him get away with treating you the way he does.

The fact that you've put up with his behavior because you don't respect yourself may be something you've been unwilling or unable to face. If you respected yourself, you wouldn't've remained in this relationship, or allowed yourself to be treated in a manner less than you deserve.

How do you learn to respect yourself enough to choose a partner that respects you? The same way you learned to disrespect yourself enough to allow yourself to be disrespected. You came to the point you're at by repeating (mostly subconsciously) to yourself the reasons you don't deserve to be respected until you were convinced by them (such as, perhaps, thinking it's worth suffering disrespect to keep him in the home with your son). Now you must consciously think of the reasons you deserve to be respected and rehearse those reasons until you've become convinced by them. You'll know when you've arrived at realizing that you deserve to be respected when you respond to being disrespected by refusing it the first time it happens and no longer tolerating it.

In the meantime, it's time for you to let this relationship go. As Marilyn Monroe said, "It's better to be unhappy alone than unhappy with someone." Spend time with yourself, without the negative reinforcement and disrespect of your partner, and learn to be happy alone. Once you've learned self-happiness and have become a whole person alone, you'll only settle for someone else who's whole and doesn't need to put someone down in order to try to feel better about themselves.

You may ask yourself, "What about our son?" Should you stay with your fiancé for the sake of your son? I want you to think about two things before you answer this question. First, is it better for your son to be raised in a house where the father doesn't love and respect the mother? Is yours the relationship that you want to model for him? Because no matter what sacrifices you make to stay in a two-parent household, your son's going to learn how to be a parent based on what he sees from both of you. Is yours the example you want for him? Second, your son's going to learn how to treat his partner based on the way he sees your fiancé treat you. Is that what you want for him and his future partner? The best gift you can give your son is for him to see you happy, fulfilled, and loved.

THIRTY-FIVE

I must comfort my girlfriend every time I tell her that something she did made me sad.

*W*hen I tell my girlfriend that something she said or did makes me sad, she starts getting sad, and I end up having to comfort her each time. It's gotten to the point that I no longer tell her when she makes me sad, because I know the tables will turn, and I'll have to end up comforting her again.

What do I do?

What she's doing is invalidating your words, muting your feelings, playing on your sympathies, and avoiding having to deal with your needs, by manipulating you into making her feel better about herself instead of listening to you. Please don't read too much into the word *manipulation*, though. Not all manipulation is malevolent or intentional.

She may not realize she's doing this. Making you sad may make her feel like she failed you, and it may truly drive her to an emotional crisis. She may be afraid that you'll abandon her, catastrophizing your sadness into her own fear that the relationship is in jeopardy.

She may have abandonment issues, and may be so afraid that you'll leave her, as so many have done throughout her life, that the possibility that something she does makes you sad overwhelms her to the point where she can't see past her own feelings to acknowledge yours.

What do you do? Instead of consoling her, **assure her that your sadness doesn't represent the end of the relationship**. This is something you should do before anything happens to make you sad—when you both are in a good place. Make sure she understands that your being sad doesn't mean that she's in danger of being abandoned. Assure her of your intention to be with her for the long term, over and over, before this situation occurs again.

Also, make sure to use "I" statements when discussing your sadness, taking responsibility for feeling sad while describing the behavior she does that creates the sadness. For example, instead of saying, "You make me sad," say "I feel sad when you do *this* or *that*." Give her responsibility for her behavior, but take responsibility for your sadness, and make sure that you don't make your sadness her fault.

Finally, the next time she becomes despairingly sad when you express your sadness, mention that you will help her with her sadness after she helps you with yours, since you were the one to bring up sadness in the first place. Walk away if she doesn't, letting her know you need some time, assure her you'll return when you feel better, and when you return, return to communicating your sadness and your need for her to help you deal with it. If she's still not ready, acting inconsolable, take another break, and keep doing so until she realizes she won't get the reward she's used to, but will have to deal with your sadness before you let the subject go.

THIRTY-SIX

How do you heal from toxic relationships?

I've been feeling down. One of the reasons is because of a toxic relationship I got out of with a narcissist. I've been trying to open myself up to dating, but I haven't had any luck. My confidence is quite low.

Sometimes I feel fine, but recently I've been quite down about it. I've tried dating apps, but I'm not having any luck on them, and I believe I'm not attractive to women.

Everyone around me is either getting engaged or married. I'm happy for them, but at the same time, it's making me feel even more alone, as it feels as though I have no one.

I've tried being positive, but I'm suffering inside to the point where I feel like it's the same thing every day. My confidence is low, and I feel lonely sometimes. I'm determined to turn my life around, but now I just feel stuck, as I don't know what to do to make my life better. I'm committed to turning my life around, but I just don't know where to start.

It's your thoughts about yourself and your situation that are causing your unhappiness. **Change your thoughts, and your emotions will change.** And the way we change our thoughts is not simply by replacing our old thoughts with new ones, which is important, but even more importantly, you must challenge your old thoughts.

What does it mean to challenge your old thoughts? It means to sit with yourself, figure out which of your thoughts are causing you to feel the way you do, write them down so you're not distracted from remembering these bad thoughts, and then challenge their validity.

I'll create some instances that I've noticed based on your story.

You say, "I feel down because I got out of a toxic relationship with a narcissist." Would ending a toxic relationship make things worse for you, or better? It would make most people feel better, since they are no longer subjected to the toxicity. Why would it make *you* feel down? Is it because you still want to be in the relationship? If so, why? Do you feel that's what you deserve? Do you believe that it's the best you can do because you're so unattractive to women? Or is it because you realize that you feel so badly about yourself that you ended up with someone who was toxic? If so, what do you plan to do about it?

You say you've been trying to open yourself up to dating but have had no luck. For which of these have you had no luck—opening yourself to dating, or being able to find someone to date? This question is important because you don't want to spend time answering a question you're not even asking yourself. If you've had no luck finding someone who'd like to date you, which is what I suspect you're saying based on other remarks you make later, I would advise you to also create opportunities to find someone outside of using dating apps, such as community events or clubs. Let others get to know you, and let yourself get to know others, up close and in real life. Of course, you *must* consider yourself worthy to be loved, and you won't do that if you haven't learned to love yourself first.

Learning to love yourself doesn't come from simply being positive or trying to think positively about yourself—learning to love yourself comes by challenging the negative things you say to yourself about yourself—things you've learned to believe because others have said them to you, you've agreed with them, and you've internalized *their* beliefs to the point where they've become *your* beliefs. One great way to challenge your negative thoughts about yourself is to simply ask why you believe what you do—in other words, what evidence is there that what you believe about yourself is true?

For instance, why is your confidence low? Is it because you've been rejected, or is it because you've taken criticism as rejection instead of opportunities to learn? Is it because you've accepted the negative things others have said about you instead of evaluating those things, learning where you need to improve and discarding the rest?

Is it true that *everyone* around you is getting engaged or married? That's impossible, but you create misery for yourself by believing it. However many are getting engaged or married, there are so many more dealing with relationship problems, or even deciding neither to be engaged nor to marry. If you believe that you're alone in neither being engaged nor married, you again create your own misery. Challenge that belief with the truth.

You put pressure on yourself to be where you believe you should be in life, rather than accepting where you are. That pressure causes your misery. Consider this: whether you accept where you are right now in life or you don't, it doesn't change where you are—it just changes how you feel about it, and attitude is everything!

You've used the word "luck" a couple of times, implying that some aspect of your future is out of your hands. The only thing that's out of your hands is the length of your life—never the depth. Your quality of life is entirely up to you, and if you're willing to make the hard choices to dig deeply into your emotional pain, sitting with it as you sort through what you can and can't change, accepting what you can't change while changing whatever you can, the quality of your life will become so much better. Unlike luck, this healing isn't done by chance; it's done by choice.

In the meantime, start to turn your life around by learning to love yourself. Take yourself out on dates. Appreciate the amazing beauty of nature and the world. Learn to enjoy your own company, and as you do, you will become someone whose company others enjoy.

THIRTY-SEVEN

I don't want to speak to my husband. I'm not sure what my next step should be.

*M*y husband is a medical student, and I'm a law student. We live in different states because of school. We have three children (a four-year-old, a three-year-old, and a nine-month-old), the children live with me, and my husband comes on the weekends to help (two nights).

Each week he comes over, on the first night, he stays up all night to have sex. On the second night, he only wants to go to sleep. He barely talks about anything and puts no energy or effort into anything. I explained to him how I feel, which he thinks is "illogical," because we're married and have kids. I feel used. It's crazy, but it's how I feel. He does help a lot when he comes, but those are also his kids and I do it alone five days a week. That's the least he can do. When it comes to me, though, I feel so alone.

I'm exhausted all week. I breastfeed all night, wake up early, dress the kids and take them to daycare, drive directly to my school, and leave school when it's time to pick them up. Dinner, snacks, baths, bedtime routine, then once they're in bed, I clean, pack their lunches, shower, and go to bed. Meanwhile, he does rotations for 4-5 hours a day, and then can do whatever he wants for the rest of the day. And he can't find the energy to stay up to spend time with me unless he's having sex.

I've been so hurt and refuse to speak to him anymore. I have already communicated how I feel and was told that it's invalid. I just don't know what to do next. I've thought about divorce a lot, but I can't pinpoint the actual reason.

You've spent a lot of time thinking about divorce because you feel neglected, disrespected, unheard, and taken for granted. Your feelings are completely valid, you're not illogical, and it sounds like what you need to do is set boundaries with him. Let him know that he can't be the only one getting what he wants out of this relationship, that you've been thinking of divorcing him, that it hurts you when he treats your feelings and thoughts as if they don't matter, and that either you will be heard, respected, romanced, and listened to, or he won't get the only thing he seems to want from you (i.e., sex) and you will act on your thoughts about divorce. It's commendable that you've attempted to communicate your feelings and thoughts to him, though he's disregarded them so far, but realize that the only chance your marriage has is if you continue to do so, regardless of his reaction.

In the meantime, examine yourself. How much of what you feel is based on exaggeration (e.g., "he stays up *all night* to have sex" and "I breastfeed *all night*"), or awfulizing (such as thinking 'nothing can be worse than what I'm experiencing with him', or 'this situation is insurmountable')? How much of what you think about this situation is factually true? What are you telling yourself about the situation that is causing excess pain, and can changing what you tell yourself about it ease some of your pain?

Meanwhile, **your husband has a lot of growing up to do.** It sounds like he's used to having his childhood freedom and doesn't want to let go of the fantasy of doing what he wants, when he wants.

Why can't you have family members watch your children for a couple of hours so you both can have some alone time together on the weekends? It'll give you an opportunity to talk about the things that are important to you and will help preserve the relationship. Tell him that he needs to make the arrangements. If he values your marriage, he'll do it, and show how much he values you, your feelings, and your needs. That'll be a great place to start.

THIRTY-EIGHT

I'm in a weird situation, and I don't understand it.

*H*e and I dated back in 2017 and again last October. Things didn't work out, but we stayed friends, and we're in the same friends' circle, which includes our families.

Last week, he invited me over to his place to drink and sleep over with his friends there (three other couples and us). I went. Things happened, he said he missed me a lot since our breakup, and talked about how he never stops thinking of me. He said he wishes this time it would work out, and his friends were very supportive as well. We slept together (not sexually), and everything was great, we got breakfast, etc.

A few days later, I texted him asking what that night meant. He said that he was tipsy, he didn't expect the night to go that way, and he was sorry if he gave me the wrong idea. We both decided to remain friends once again.

Fast forward to a couple of days ago. I posted a new guy I'm dating on Facebook, and my friend unfollowed me. I'm confused as to why, when *he said he didn't want anything romantic and that it was a drunken mistake. I asked him, and he said it's hard for him not to think of me while seeing my posts.*

Did I do anything wrong? I still don't understand him at all. Please help.

There is a Latin phrase that lends itself very well to what happened: *in vino veritas*. It translates, "In wine, there is truth," and it suggests that a person under the influence of alcohol is more likely to voice their true feelings and desires. It explains what happened the night you stayed over. He was drinking alcohol, his defense mechanisms were down, the fear he would've normally had in telling you the truth went away as he imbibed liquid courage, and he told the truth about how he feels.

He hoped you would declare your feelings so that he could feel safe declaring his, and when you didn't (at least I didn't see where you said you felt the same way), he backtracked so he wouldn't look vulnerable. He wasn't honest with you about how he felt and was afraid to be at that point. As a result, he sent mixed messages, so you asked him where things were going, and he refused to acknowledge how he truly felt. Instead, he denied his feelings about you, and you believed him, as you should've.

Did you do anything wrong? Absolutely not. **It's not up to you to wrestle honesty out of anyone.** They choose whether to be honest about their feelings and thoughts, and your acceptance of his words as truth isn't a mistake. I say this with a warning, though. If you felt something for him, it doesn't sound like you acknowledged it, either. It seems like you had feelings for him and would've taken the relationship to the next level had he been willing to be honest about his feelings. Preparing to love is about honesty, beginning with being honest with yourself. Instead of asking him what the night meant to him, you could've led the conversation by describing what the night meant to you. Again, it's not wrong that you didn't, but understanding him isn't as important as understanding yourself, and understanding yourself begins with self-honesty.

THIRTY-NINE

He broke up with me, and now asks us to be friends with benefits.

We dated for around 5-6 years. He cheated on me, and recently said he wants to end things between us. He also said he wants us to have a friend with benefits relationship. He told me to stay single, and he and I can have a lot of physical fun, which I won't get if I date someone else.

What is he saying? What does he want?

He said *exactly* what he wanted—to have his cake and eat it, too. He wants you to remain single so he can have access to you anytime he wants, but he also wants to be with other women. I'm not sure if the physical fun you won't have if you date someone else means that he won't allow you to have "fun" with him if you date someone else, or that he thinks no one else can provide "physical fun" like he can.

Whatever he meant, the real question is this: what do *you* want? Do you want to share him with other women? Do you believe you're not worth having a faithful, monogamous man? Do you think a cheater provides you with the relationship you deserve? Or do you love yourself enough to insist on what you need from a relationship, refusing to settle for less?

If you're even considering his offer, it's a sign that you love yourself less than you deserve. If you love yourself less than you deserve, you'll be attracted to people who love you less than you deserve. You're worth more than being a "friends with benefits" for someone who ended things with you. I hope you believe that, too.

FORTY

My boyfriend is smothering me. What do I do?

I've been with my boyfriend for eight months. We were very much in love up until about three months ago, when he started having financial issues. He accepted a new job that doesn't pay very well. Since then, I've been providing for us, and he asks me for money most weeks when he falls short. He says he feels bad about it, and he does pay me back when he can.

I've started to notice that his hygiene isn't the best (sometimes he smells down below), and his room can be an absolute mess. Lately when we've had sex, I've been finding myself just wanting it to be over. It's always the same moves, and he likes it rough most of the time.

I was so in love with this guy, and I want back what we had when we met. I'm sitting here wondering if I was just so blinded by meeting a guy who was so interested in me from the start—no mind games. Now he expects us to spend every weekend together, messages me several times *throughout the day, and constantly talks about us moving in together, and all I can think is "I need space."*

I feel terrible. He's a beautiful person with the most genuine heart. I want to make this work, but don't know how to have an honest conversation about what bothers me. Help.

It sounds like your boyfriend is depressed and desperate for reassurance. It began when he started having financial issues and ended up taking the lower paying job. Instead of being able to, I suspect, "be the man," he had to rely on you to help meet his financial obligations, which he allowed to make him feel like less than a real man. This is what he means when he says he feels bad about having to borrow money from you.

Feeling emasculated can morph into depression, with accompanying symptoms—decreased self-care (to include hygiene), withdrawal from people (while desperately clinging to you), less interest in things, self-depreciation or guilt that can evolve into feeling helpless, trouble with sexual performance, etc. At the same time, he senses your emotional distance, which frightens him, and he's awkwardly trying to remedy it by trying to spend more time and increase contact with you, which drives you to the point where all you want right now is space.

You sense his emotional burden, and while you want to communicate your needs, you don't feel he has the space to hear you when he seems so overwhelmed by his own issues. Now you've moved from "we were very much in love" to "I *was* so in love with this guy", but you also say you want to make this work. So do you *really* want to be in a romantic relationship with him, or has that time passed? If you want to be in a relationship with him because he's a "beautiful person" with a "generous heart", then what you may be looking for is a relationship with someone with those qualities, since you didn't mention that you wanted to make this work because you still love him.

You can appreciate the person he is without being in a romantic relationship with him. **Take some time to decide what it is you really want, and let your actions follow that decision.** If you decide you want to keep the relationship with him, I suggest you both enter therapy together, where a therapist can help you hear each other and sort through the subjective noise that becomes inherent in all relationships. If you don't, you owe it to both of you to be honest with him about it as soon as possible.

FORTY-ONE

I feel like a failure after a date with a guy whom I really liked.

*L*ast weekend, I had a first date with a guy with whom I matched quite some time ago, and before the date we talked a lot, which eventually led to the date. Our date was amazing on both sides—we were open and relaxed around each other, and there were no feelings of discomfort or awkwardness. We walked and talked for several hours, cuddled, and left with a small kiss on the cheek.

During our date, we exchanged items to return later (a book from me and a T-shirt from him). I must admit that during our date I never felt so great and that I fit so well with someone else my entire life, and I was eagerly looking forward to another date.

On Tuesday, he told me he'd love to go either to the cinema or café, where we could cuddle and spend some time together, so we arranged the second date for Friday. Except yesterday evening he wrote me a message saying he'd like to move our date to the weekend or even later. He then tried to explain that he felt like we were moving way too fast and got *too emotionally attached while not knowing each other for long. He also mentioned that the reason he moved that date was because he needed to meet with someone else before me. He told me that besides me, he's been talking with other women, he would like to first get his head straight, and for now that we should stay as friends.*

I felt heartbroken and hurt but accepted the deal before going to sleep. I've been feeling a bit better, but still bummed about the sudden change of events and everything he told me. I feel like a failure, and I that I must've done something, despite him reassuring me that there was no fault in me whatsoever.

I'm willing to talk and take it slowly, but I still feel extremely hurt after everything.

I don't know what to do or what to think. I don't want to cut all contact with him at all, but at the same time I feel that if we were to remain only as friends, I would suffer a lot and would never be happy.

One of the most natural things we do as humans, because it appears to have low emotional risk, is to assume that another person feels the positive things we feel for them. Because the date went so well, you assumed that you both were equally into each other, which was a normal, though incomplete, way to assess the get-together. Conversely, one of the hardest things we can do is ask someone how they interpret where they stand with us, because that opens us up to rejection. What you took away from the date was something that's common to do, because we tend to see things in a way that makes us feel safe and loved, whenever possible. **The scary, but necessary thing to do, is to ask how the other person experienced the connection between the two of you.**

It's said that people can only meet you as deeply as they've met themselves, and he seems like someone who's afraid to meet another deeply. That's typical for someone who has been emotionally hurt. He shows the signs of being emotionally unavailable, to include backing away from you after the wonderful experience you describe between the two of you and talking to other women. The fact that he's made himself emotionally unavailable isn't your fault. His reassurance that it was not your fault is the truth. He realizes that it's not you; it's him. You didn't fail—in fact, you've shown that you're emotionally available. Where you display behavior that hurts you, rather, is in believing that you'll suffer a lot and never be happy if you can't have a romantic relationship with him.

Besides the fact that no one can so precisely predict the future, where's the evidence that you'll suffer a lot and never be happy if you can't be in a romantic relationship with him? The fact that you've tied the future of your happiness to him so intricately after only one date shows you may be dealing with attachment insecurity and fear of abandonment, which may come from inconsistent positive emotional responses from your caregivers as you were growing up, which caused you to lack trust that your emotional needs would be met. You've met someone who seems like he could meet your emotional needs; however, he said that he's not ready to do so, and you seriously doubt you'll meet someone else who will.

If you're not yet at the place where you can be happy if you and he were to remain friends, it's best that you let him know that you aren't able to maintain a friendship with him and work to find happiness with yourself. If you can't find happiness with yourself first, you won't be able to find true happiness with anyone else. In order to find happiness with yourself, you must find yourself worthy to love you. That will mean dealing with the rejections of the past, deciding that any rejection of you doesn't mean that you're a reject, and understanding that people that offhandedly reject others have first rejected themselves. Then decide you won't be included in those that reject you. Find reasons that you're lovable and worthy to be loved and love yourself for those reasons. As self-love emanates from you, you'll become happy, and you'll attract true love from others.

Forty-Two

How do I get my boyfriend to understand how to comfort me?

*M y boyfriend and I always ask each other, "Do you want com-
fort or solutions?" when it comes to venting about our problems
to each other. I'm usually pretty good at being able to do both, but my
boyfriend seems unable to ever give me comfort.*

*I ask him to just listen to me and provide dialogue, instead of a
one-sided conversation where I do all the talking and he just sits there,
and that I don't want him to fix my problems, but every time, I wind
up talking to a brick wall of "oh, that sucks," "okay," or "damn." This
doesn't help me at all, and I wonder how I can show him how to comfort
me more effectively.*

*The ways that I've told him just don't seem to work for him. There's
just something about him, or men in general, that I need to understand
myself. I don't know, but I do know that I need help.*

As you've observed, men are solution oriented. That doesn't mean that he can't learn to comfort, though.

It's clear that he understands the value of supplying comfort, since he also answers your question about giving him either comfort or solutions. You may ask him why does he need comfort sometimes. Use the answers he supplies to help him understand why you need it, too.

One of the best ways you can teach him to supply comfort is to show that he's actively listening to you. Some ways he can do that include: making sure he doesn't interrupt you because he thinks he understands the problem you describe, but waits for pauses to ask questions; show he's interested by asking you questions that indicate he wants to understand your point of view; offer you verbal cues such as asking, "what happened?" or "tell me more" or "I really want to understand"; and paraphrasing or summarizing the things you've said to show that he's listening and really understands.

He's offering blanket feedback that's easy and doesn't require true listening, which you can see through very easily. He needs to make more of an investment in listening to you. Knowing that you're listened to will provide you with some of the comfort you seek.

[As a side note: **men who are only interested in listening to women when they think they'll get sex out of it are a disappointing turn-off to women.** Guys, we can do better than that.]

FORTY-THREE

How do you process the fact that they will be out of your life forever after a breakup?

I can't stop thinking about the fact that I'll lose my best friend, lover, and the one who was the most important person in my life...forever. It feels like I'm mourning a death. I'm jealous that they're still in the lives of others but can't be in mine.

I don't want them to be a memory. I already have abandonment issues, so this realization totally breaks me. I feel like I can't go on.

How do you process this—especially when you believe the breakup was your fault? How do you cope?

A breakup is a loss, which is a type of death—a death which you are mourning. And just as you have no power over another's death turning into memories of being with them, you have no control over this relationship becoming no more than memories. You process the demise of this relationship the same way you process the death of someone you love.

You feel the hole in your heart and in your life. It seems insurmountable, overwhelming, catastrophic, unyielding, and unending. You have debilitating, gut-wrenching moans and floods of tears. You feel lost, desperate, unmoored, untethered. You don't know how you'll go on. You're consumed with grief and regret. There seems to be nothing but clouds and rain overhead. And then, somewhere down the road, a single ray of sunshine peeks from behind a cloud for just a moment. At some further, undetermined point, that sunbeam lasts a bit longer. The next time, even longer. You catch yourself smiling briefly. Then a little longer. The next time, even longer.

You'll never be the same, but that's not a bad thing—it's a *better* thing. **It's the reason a funeral is better than a party.** Loss makes us reflect on our lives. In those moments, we take them less for granted, and we take others less for granted. We appreciate life so much more.

As for how you deal with feeling at fault for the breakup, you do it by accepting what has happened. Even if you had you done something differently, you wouldn't't've been guaranteed a different outcome. You can do everything "right" and still experience a breakup. The only guaranteed outcomes we have are those of the past, which is unchangeable; the present, which is influenced by so many things that it can't be accurately predicted; and the future, which is unknown. You deal with this by accepting that you did the best you could with what you knew at the time, and you were dealing with abandonment issues and the fears that came from that, which caused you to respond the way you did. From there, you work on those issues, realize that you're worthy of love and of not being abandoned, prove it by loving yourself and not abandoning the idea that you're worthy of this love, and accept from another the love and acceptance you've finally given yourself.

FORTY-FOUR

My girlfriend doesn't prioritize me but gets mad when I can't see her.

*T*his started a few months ago. I know my girlfriend is busy and has a lot on her plate, but she also expresses that she wants to spend time with me. I **never** complain when she goes out with other people or does other things that don't involve me. But it's sad seeing how often she goes out with her friends, and how she puts more effort into meeting them than me.

As of late, I have taken a lot of extra shifts at work to keep myself occupied, and it just so happens that a couple of those shifts are during times where she doesn't have anything to do. So she has gotten mad at me for taking those shifts instead of making sure I can meet her.

In her words, "Why do you always gotta work when I have time to meet you?" Is that fair? Am I supposed to be free anytime she wants, or should it go both ways?

The only reason I worry about this is that my whole life revolves around her and has for the last two years. I'm lonely outside of the relationship, and I'm worried it wouldn't get any better if it ends between us.

The fact that your entire life revolves around her is a red flag. You must know that it shouldn't, and that there's something wrong with it, so what will you do about it?

So far, what you've been doing is trying to keep yourself occupied at work by taking more shifts, and one of the reasons for this is so you don't have to think about missing her, and so you don't have to face your loneliness when she's not around. But think about this: if the two of you were able to spend more time together, and you got to choose what both of you would do, what would you choose? Whatever it is, try doing it on your own instead of taking extra shifts. This way, some of your life will revolve around you creating your own happiness.

Another reason you may be taking shifts that end up occurring when she's free is because you resent her putting more effort into being with others, and it's your passive aggressive way of communicating this, since you never complain when she goes out with people or do other things that don't involve you. Passive aggressiveness is an ineffective form of communication. It's much better to sit her down and tell her exactly how you feel. Don't think of it as complaining. If you don't tell her what you need, you can't blame her for not meeting that need. Don't allow pride or ego to tell you that she should know, and that she would realize what she's doing if she cared. You'll know how much she cares after you tell her what you need. If she works on meeting your need, she shows that she cares, and if she doesn't, she doesn't.

Are you supposed to be free anytime she wants? No, and she's not supposed to be free anytime you want. That's not how life works. There are times you both will be unable to break away from something, and it's unfair, impractical, and illogical for either of you to demand unhindered, 24-hour access to each other.

Love yourself enough to ask for what you need, and if she's unwilling or unable to give it to you, love yourself enough to enjoy your own company until you find the right person for you.

FORTY-FIVE

My girlfriend complains about gaining weight but doesn't want my help.

*M*y girlfriend has gained over 110 pounds in the three years *we've* been together. She complains almost every day about *being overweight and has a full meltdown at least once a week about it. She told me that I needed to help her lose weight, but when I tried, she told me I was controlling her.*

The weight isn't the issue for me—it's the meltdowns about it, followed by overeating because she doesn't feel full yet. Like she would cry and yell at me for her weight, and then I'd make her dinner, but she wouldn't be full, so she'd make herself another dinner, and then eat a two-pound tub of chocolate pudding.

Now I've started noticing she isn't taking proper care of her hygiene, especially with showering and brushing her teeth. I don't want to see her as gross, but I can't help it. Please give me some advice.

Your girlfriend sees herself as gross, believing that hygiene won't improve her appeal, and is depressed about her weight, but feels like she's caught up in a helpless cycle of overeating, followed by guilt, followed by more overeating, followed by more guilt, etc. She's addicted to food, which is why she asks for your help but doesn't really seem to want it. Think of any other type of addiction, and you'll see the same behaviors displayed in her actions.

She hates herself, and doesn't understand how you can love her, since she finds herself so unlovable, so she's subconsciously trying to repel you and cause you to reject her by not showering and brushing her teeth.

The weight may not be an issue for you, but it's certainly an issue for her. **She knows that she's responsible for her weight gain but feels powerless when it comes to food.**

I recommend that you suggest to her that she goes to therapy or a support group to work on her reasons for overeating. She may be emotionally eating to cover up feelings brought on by past trauma, choosing the euphoria that comes from overeating over those feelings. That past trauma may also cause her to want to be unattractive, so she won't be taken advantage of again. She may be gaining weight to feel more powerful and in control of her life because she was made to feel powerless by a trusted family member or friend of the family when she was a young girl. The control she feels in the portions of food she eats may give her a feeling of security. Whatever the reason, if she's willing to deal with it, she will be able to overcome her addiction to food, get her life back, and become emotionally healthy, which will allow her to become physically healthy.

FORTY-SIX

I lied about hoarding chocolate, and he won't forgive me.

I *have a habit of buying chocolate and hiding it in my closet because, to be honest, I hate to share it. Stupid, I know, but it's become a pattern.*

When he found out I did this, he got angry, said he was hurt, and I said I would stop. I did for a while, but then he started making remarks about my buying chocolate (which he now saw because it wasn't hidden), and that really annoyed me. So I hid some again.

Today, while I was out, he decided to go through my closet and find my stash. When he confronted me, I lied and said that it was old, and continued to lie when he told me that he had gone through it before and it wasn't there, and I kept trying to deny it by blaming it on someone else. In the end, of course, I admitted it (way too late), and asked him to forgive me and said I was deeply sorry and felt so guilty for doing it, which was true. He told me he's disgusted by me and my behavior, that

*he can't believe a single word that comes out of my mouth, and that he
will never trust me again.*

*I've apologized a million times, and feel bad for doing it, but he will
not forgive me. I know that he's right, but I feel that the treatment he's
giving me is punishment, and that he's been going through my stuff just
to catch me red-handed. I'm in the wrong, I know, but deep down I feel
like he wanted to catch me doing something, so he has a right to be angry
at me and not talk to me while I continue to beg for forgiveness. (He has
previously gone through my phone and has admitted going through my
stuff on more than one occasion.)*

*I'd love to know what you think I should do. The guilt is really killing
me.*

He's overreacting and not taking the reason you hide chocolate
into account. In fact, he doesn't care about the *why*—he takes very
personally what has nothing to do with him. Have *you* thought about
why you hoard chocolate? There must be a reason.

You shouldn't've promised to stop. Instead, you should've asked
him to be patient with you while you figure out why you do this.
Also, you should've communicated that his making remarks about
your chocolate when you no longer hid it was annoying (and hurtful),
instead of hiding it again because you felt that way. In other words,
it's best to communicate your feelings with your partner, rather than
defaulting to behavior that makes you feel safe but ashamed.

He did want to catch you, so he'd have a reason to be angry. He
kept searching through your closet. This shows that he expected, even
wanted, to catch you hiding chocolate. Why would you doing this
even be important to him? He has a self-prophetic notion that you're
untrustworthy. That's the way he sees you, and he won't stop looking

for evidence for this until he proves that what he believes is right. That's called confirmation bias.

And why does he feel the need to continually go through your things? This shows, again, that he never trusted you and wouldn't stop until he proved himself right. He goes through your phone—why? To see if you're hiding chocolates? No. To see if you're cheating on him. He doesn't trust you, and he's trying to justify his insecurity by using your hidden chocolate.

You believe that he's punishing you because that's exactly what he's doing. He was probably cheated on in his past and has brought that baggage into your relationship. Now that you feel guilty, he can punish you at leisure for what someone else did to him.

The question is this—what will you do about it? Since you know that trust doesn't exist in your relationship, it's reasonable to assume that what you thought was a loving relationship isn't, because you must trust someone to have that kind of love for them. Until he's willing to deal with his issues, he can't function in a romantic relationship, with you or anyone else. If you try to keep this level of relationship with him, you'll only hurt yourself. The best thing you can do for yourself is to realize that he's not ready for this kind of relationship, let him go, and allow each of you to work on your issues.

Learn why you have the fear that causes you to hide chocolate. It sounds like it could've been caused by the trauma of poverty. If that's the case, the work consists of reminding yourself, as many times as you need to, that there's always more at the store, and whereas you didn't have the means to have it whenever you wanted it before, you do now. Let go of the poverty thinking brought on by the past and learn to live in the plenteous present.

I know what this is like. I had to eat out of city garbage cans growing up, so I understand the work it takes to break out of that mentality, even when you can afford food. **Hoarding chocolate may also be an attempt to control your future, in that you can trust that it will always be there, unlike other things and people in your life.** These are all things to consider as you continue your journey in learning to love yourself. I wish you well.

FORTY-SEVEN

Why do I think of my boyfriend's ex-girlfriend so often, and how do I let it go?

*M*y boyfriend and I have been together for almost two years. I know he loves me, and I love him very much. He doesn't even look at other girls (at least not in front of me) and hasn't done anything to make me feel insecure about our relationship.

I think about his ex-girlfriend, and more generally past girls he's been with, often—maybe once a day. I don't know why. It could be because when we first met as friends, they were together, and he at one point told me he thought he'd marry her one day but that, at the moment, he wasn't so sure.

Flash forward to a month or so later, and he's actively pursuing me and telling me he broke up with her. This was over two years ago, but I think just knowing that he jumped from that relationship to ours so quickly, in a span of four months, and that at one point he thought he'd marry her, is making me think about her and compare myself to her.

Why is this happening? And how do I let go of this?

When you say you compare yourself to her, this is what I hear: just as he says he loved his ex, he says he loves you; just as he planned to marry her, he may one day plan to marry you; just as he broke up with her after professing deep love for her, he may break up with you after professing deep love for you. These things may be true, or they may be different with you—you just don't know, and you can't think of any reason it would be different with you.

You're thinking, "Why did he leave her? And will he leave me one day for the same reason?"

There's only one way to let go of this—talk about it with him. Let him know the thoughts with which you struggle. Let him know that you feel insecure about your relationship with him. Ask him why he broke up with her. Ask him what the difference is between your relationship with him and the ones he was in before. Ask him how he feels about the relationship with you. Ask him what his intentions are for your relationship. Allow him to reassure you.

Of course, there's the chance that he'll tell you things you don't want to hear. He may say things that will hurt you—deeply—which could cause you to be afraid to ask these questions. But wherever he is in the relationship, and however it compares to relationships in the past, it's better that you know sooner than later, instead of tormenting yourself with thoughts that may or may not be true. You say that you know he loves you, but if you did, you wouldn't be tormented with these thoughts. And if you're afraid of asking these questions, think of it this way—would you rather be tortured by thoughts which aren't true, or would you rather know the truth?

And why should you do this? Because **you deserve to love yourself enough to know the truth.** You deserve to love yourself enough to be assured that his love is real, constant, and special, or to find love that is if his is not.

FORTY-EIGHT

After I cheated on my wife, she refuses to have orgasms with me.

I'm confused, because it should be the other way around.

I cheated on my wife once. I couldn't live with the guilt, so I told her. It took us over two years to reconcile. Eventually, we started having sex again.

Now, for six months, we have had sex at least twice a week. The only thing is that she never lets me pleasure her anymore. She does all the stuff I like for me, but she refuses to receive. I asked her once about it, and she played confused and said she was satisfied with our sex life, so I needn't worry. But I know she's not orgasming because she doesn't allow me to do any of the stuff she loves. She insists that I have my orgasm before her, and then she pretends that she's satisfied.

I thought it would make more sense if it was the other way around, because I'm the one who cheated and should be punished. That she should want fulfillment and to ignore my needs. Why is she doing this?

This has nothing to do with punishment, and everything to do with trust.

A man can argue with a woman one minute, never resolve the argument, and want to have sex with her, culminating in an orgasm, the next. This is inconceivable for most women.

You may ask what does this have to do with your question. The answer is everything.

As men, we compartmentalize our lives in such a way that we conclude that an argument is an argument, sex is sex, and the twain don't ever have to meet. We reason that we'll have amazing sex now and finish the argument later, if we need to. Men's hearts don't have to be involved at all in order to have an orgasm.

What I found to be true for most woman, however, is that their orgasms are tied to her minds and to their hearts. The way that it was once explained to me by a woman was that her vagina is tied to her heart. Her vagina, her mind, and her heart must be in sync for her to allow you to bring her to an orgasm. If she doesn't trust you, she won't allow you to bring her to an orgasm, because an orgasm for her represents vulnerability, surrender, and trust.

There are things still troubling her about your actions, and since that's true, her heart, mind, and vagina won't be in sync regarding you.

If she's still dealing with issues surrounding your infidelity, she won't surrender herself to you in orgasm. You may be tired of talking about it, you may want to put it in the past, you may no longer want to deal with it, but it hasn't been resolved in her heart or mind. She may have sex with you for your fulfillment to minimize the chance that you'll stray again, but that doesn't mean she trusts you.

If you want her to allow you to bring her to orgasm, you must solve this issue the way she needs it to be resolved, instead

of avoiding it. You may know that you won't do it again, but she doesn't, and until you do whatever it takes to provide her that reassurance, she won't allow herself to be vulnerable enough with you to accept an orgasm from you.

Ask her how she's dealing with finding out about your infidelity. Ask her what still needs to be discussed and be willing to listen with the intent to understand, rather than the intent to reply. Don't interrupt, don't justify your actions, don't turn the tables and discuss any of her problem behaviors. This isn't *your* time, and you can't attempt to dominate the conversation in any way and expect things to be resolved. Be willing to discuss this as many times as she needs. Don't act exasperated or impatient because the issue hasn't been resolved in her mind and heart yet. Show whatever patience you need to show—after all, she deserves it.

When she trusts that she can deal with this situation with you without any impatience on your part, and she trusts that you remain willing to love her through her fears and patiently reassure her, she'll slowly open her heart completely to you again, and once she trusts you, she'll allow you to bring her to orgasm.

FORTY-NINE

My (ex-) boyfriend of four years cheated on me, and I feel unloved and incapable of being loved.

*W**e dated for almost four years. I cut him off a couple of weeks ago after we got into a big argument, when he told me that he didn't regret abusing me physically and verbally. Came to find out he's been cheating on me, and he started dating the other girl as soon as we cut things off.*

I feel so empty and unlovable, I don't know why I'm so angry, and why I feel like I want him back, even after everything. I feel like I'm not only incapable of being loved, but of loving. What do I do?

It sounds like the abuse has been going on throughout the relationship and, though in the past he may have apologized for it, he's now willing to admit that he really wasn't sorry for treating you that way. You could've realized that he really wasn't sorry, even when he was apologizing for it, because he continued the behaviors. You allowed him to continue to treat you that way as long as he said he was sorry but was unwilling to allow it to continue once he said he didn't regret it. (I assume that he said he was sorry in the past because it hit you so hard when he finally said he didn't regret it.)

If by "cutting things off" you mean that you broke up with him, his dating someone else isn't cheating; but if by "cutting things off" you mean withholding sex, you were trying to use it to manipulate him into feeling sorry for his behavior. If so, how sorry would he really have been? How would you know he was sorry if it was possible that he was just saying what he needed to say in order to be able to have sex with you? Did you just need to hear the words so much that you were willing to offer sex to hear them? Again, this is only the case if you were trying to use the offer of sex to get him to express remorse.

You may have felt empty and unlovable before you cut him off but was able to ignore those feelings as long as you could count on the fact that you *had* a boyfriend, and you may have used him to prove to yourself that your feelings were wrong, but now that he's your ex, you must face feelings that were already there.

I believe you're angry because of a combination of things. First, by (most likely) asking yourself things like "How could he do this to me? How could he leave me for someone else?" and other questions for which you won't get any answers. If you could ask *him* these questions, and if he was self-insightful enough to be able to thoughtfully answer them for you, that would be one thing; however, if you're asking yourself, over and over, questions that won't get answered, you're doing yourself no good, and you're creating a loop of despair for yourself. Second, you're angry that you allowed yourself to be treated the way he's treated you for the last four years, and you haven't forgiven yourself for letting this happen to you.

You want him back because you're afraid of seeking another relationship, and you're afraid of the unknown. You have no idea if the next relationship will be worse than this last one and believe that this past relationship was bad enough that you don't want to face the possibility of things being worse. Instead, imagine if things were better in your next relationship. That's just as possible.

It's interesting that you say that you're not only incapable of being loved, but of loving. The reason for that is because you don't love yourself, you don't have the emotional space to love another, and you don't feel worthy of love. In preparing to love, the most important thing is to learn to love yourself, and then to believe yourself worthy of being loved by others.

How do you learn to love yourself? First, by forgiving yourself for all your mistakes. This is not simply waving a magic wand of words like, "I forgive myself for all my past mistakes," and suddenly guilt disappears. This is going over each thing you don't forgive yourself for, and for each thing you do the following—look at the circumstances surrounding each it; understand what you did well and what you didn't do so well; acknowledge that if you had known better, you would've done better; sit with it until you have forgiven yourself; and repeat the process with the next thing on the list.

Then you make a list of the things that are good about you and focus on that list, giving it as much time as you've given yourself in thinking about what's bad about you. No one is *all* bad, so don't give up looking for good things about yourself because it's hard. It's hard because you've made a habit out of thinking the worst about yourself, and you're now working to develop the opposite habit—thinking the best about yourself—and habits take time to develop.

Then to deal with feeling worthy to be loved, ask yourself, "Why would someone be lucky to be with me?" Make a list and be ready to continually add to that list. Once you love yourself, you'll believe that you're worthy of love, and once you believe you're worthy of love, you won't settle for anything less than true love, and you won't give do-overs to people who treat you like leftovers.

FIFTY

My girlfriend has developed a habit of being "brutally honest" with me all the time.

I have been dating my girlfriend for around eight months. I love her and all that, but she's developed this habit with me where she's "brutally honest" all the time. It's often when I'm simply looking for reassurance, which is why it's upsetting to me.

Here are a few examples of what I mean:

1. *We work together in a restaurant. I'm still learning to use the registers, and at the end of a shift I made a joke about how I'm gonna be a pro one day. She said that I sucked at it and that I shouldn't bother training on them.*

2. *I was joking around last night and just bantering with her, and she told me out of the blue that my sense of humor sucks, that I rely too much on dad jokes, and that she's never once laughed at my jokes from what she can remember.*

3. *I'm really into science fiction shows, such as Rick & Morty and Doctor Who, and she's more of a supernatural fan, so she's constantly saying my taste in shows and movies suck and always taking shots at my favorite shows.*

I know this may sound dumb, but it almost feels like she's just always looking for a reason to get her little digs in at me. It's hard for me to put into words, but it's been making me quite frustrated in the past few weeks. Any advice on what to do about this? I do love her, just not this habit she's gotten into.

She could be either projecting her crippling self-criticism onto you or picking fights to drive you away.

She seems a classic example of someone who suffers from low self-esteem and insecurity. In the beginning of your relationship, she was mindful of what she said and how she acted, while looking for you to fill the hole she feels within but was disappointed that you don't. The truth is that you can't. As I discussed in length in my last book, *Things I Wish My Father Had Told Me*, relationships don't follow the Law of Addition, but the Law of Multiplication. To briefly summarize what this means, some people seek romantic relationships as half a person looking for their other half, believing that being with that person will make them feel whole—in other words, $\frac{1}{2} + \frac{1}{2} = 1$. However, this isn't how it works by the Law of Multiplication. By that law, $\frac{1}{2} \times \frac{1}{2} = \frac{1}{4}$. So when a half person reaches out to another half person for wholeness, what is the other half person doing? Reaching out to the other person for the same thing. So you end up with two people reaching for the same thing from one another, but neither having enough to give to each other, and finally feeling like they have less than when they started the relationship.

What this means for your relationship is that she's lashing out because she feels empty enough to do so. You mention that you're looking for reassurance; so is she. Neither one of you have mentioned that that's what you want from each other, though (I assume). She's not going to provide you reassurance while she feels insecure. She doesn't have a good sense of self-worth, so she's unable to provide you with one.

I can guarantee you this—as much as she puts you down, she's worse on herself. It's the way she's programmed her mind, and she can't switch from being self-negative to *you*-positive. The mind doesn't work that way. Show me a person who's always negative, and I'll show you a person who's unable to love and accept themselves.

The solution for you both, according to this Law of Multiplication, is to become whole in yourselves. For you, that means to come to a place where you feel confident that you will become a pro at the registers, that you're comfortable with your sense of humor (while not quitting your day job), and where you are able to ignore her attempts at putting down your taste in shows. For her, it will be when she no longer feels the need to put you down or demean you in any way, because she's so satisfied with and secure in herself that all she radiates is positivity and love. This, according to the Law of Multiplication, is when 1 x 1 will equal 1.

She may also be picking fights with you to drive you away. Since you've only been frustrated for about three weeks of this eight-month relationship, it sounds like she hasn't been doing this the whole time. Or she may have been doing it the last three months, and you've gotten frustrated over the last three weeks. However long she's been doing it, if it hasn't been the whole time you and she have been together, you may want to ask her if she still wants to be in the relationship. Find out if anything's changed. Is she interested in someone else and afraid to tell you? Does she still love you? If she does, does she realize how hurtful her behavior is? Is she willing to change?

Your responsibility in this is only to yourself; you can't change her. You may suggest it, and she may balk at it, but that's all you can do. One way you may provoke her to think about changing is by asking her to consider why she feels the need to put you down and call it brutal honesty when, in fact, what she expresses isn't honesty at all—at best, it's her opinion, and at worst, it's bullying and toxic.

Finally, you may consider taking time apart, working on yourself, allowing her to work on herself, and seeing if the relationship will work after doing so. You may also consider couples' therapy, even if you decide to take time apart. I wish you well.

FIFTY-ONE

My girlfriend says that I've changed and that I make her feel insecure, because I've lost weight and have been working on myself. This kind of rubs me the wrong way, and I feel like I've outgrown her.

*M*y girlfriend and I have been together for two years and started dating in our last year of university. At the time we were dating while at university, we were both pretty laid back and didn't really do anything productive besides studying, and I also worked a part-time job. Our free time was mostly spent in bed chilling and watching Netflix or going out with a few friends.

During my time at university, I didn't really work on myself physically and mentally, but when I graduated, I started making great *money, and I had more free time. I joined a gym and got in the best shape of my life. I also upgraded my wardrobe and started putting more effort into looking good. This has also made me feel more confident and led me to make a lot of new friends. Overall, I feel like I've grown as a person this year since graduating, and I've never felt better physically and mentally.*

My girlfriend, on the other hand, hasn't really changed much since university. She started working a part-time job and does the same things we did back at university.

She recently expressed to me that all the changes I've made have made her feel insecure. She says that I don't need to change, and that things were good the way they were. When I asked her what exactly makes her feel insecure, she says it's the unnecessary changes I've made in my life. This really rubs me the wrong way.

I feel like I've changed for the good this past year and am growing as a person. I was expecting my partner to support me in this growth; instead, I feel like she's trying to hold me back. I support her with everything she does in her life, and it feels wrong that she doesn't do the same for me.

This has really made me question whether we're compatible. I won't be dialing back on my growth any time soon, and I'm continuing this trajectory for at least the next few years. And the last thing I want is to be held back by a relationship. How do you think I should deal with this situation?

This has nothing to do with you and everything to do with her.

Your growth shines a spotlight on her lack thereof, which she's uncomfortable seeing. You're at the gym; you're in the best shape of your life. You're around others interested in self-improvement. She may be thinking about the ladies you see at the gym, and what they must look like compared to her. This doesn't mean that she looks bad, of course, but that may not stop her from thinking so.

You've upgraded your wardrobe, and she may be thinking to herself, 'Who's he trying to look good for? He isn't trying to impress me, so who's he trying to impress?' She may not think you're doing it for yourself and feels jealous and insecure. When she says your changes are unnecessary, she's saying they're unnecessary for her, and part of her may wonder if they're necessary for someone else.

She may also be the crabs in your basket. What do I mean?

"Crabs in a basket" refer to a situation where a group of crabs is confined within a container or enclosure. Metaphorically, it symbolizes a scenario where she exhibits a behavior that hinders your progress or success.

In a literal sense, crabs in a basket exhibit an interesting behavior. If you place multiple crabs in a basket without a lid, you might assume that they could easily climb out. However, what actually happens is quite surprising. Whenever one crab tries to climb out of the basket, the other crabs will pull it back down, preventing its freedom. This peculiar behavior leads to a situation where none of the crabs can escape, as they hinder each other's progress.

This analogy is often used to describe situations where individuals or groups discourage or undermine the success or progress of others. It highlights the tendency for some people to resent and hinder the advancement of those who are trying to improve their circumstances or pursue their goals.

As long as you followed the routine you had before, she felt no pressure to change, but when you sought self-improvement, she may have felt that she couldn't keep up or remain interesting to you, so she's trying to drag you back down to where you were before. She may also think you'll find someone more interesting than her.

Have you encouraged her to join you at the gym or shopping, or brought home some outfits for her while you're out shopping for yourself? Besides wanting her to support you in your growth, you could encourage her, as well, to join you in your growth journey.

The unavoidable thing that people in relationships typically don't talk about, or even realize sometimes, is that the person you're with today isn't usually going to be the same person five years from now, or ten, or twenty. People in relationships *must* allow their partners to grow and be willing to grow themselves. While it does sound like she wants to stunt your maturational growth, it's also true that she's not embracing hers.

You should absolutely continue your growth and embrace the man you're becoming and will become, while encouraging her to do the same for the woman she's becoming and will become. One only need look at nature to know that change is both necessary and inevitable. Nothing stays the same. Nor should she. Let her know that she needs to embrace the person you're becoming for the relationship to continue and encourage her to set goals to accomplish for herself. Change is as inevitable for her as it is for anything else in nature. Talk to her about embracing change—in you *and* in herself.

No one should allow themselves to be held back by *any* relationship, whether friendly, familial, or romantic. If she's not willing to accept your growth and insist that you go back to the way you were, it may be time to end the relationship, but if she's willing to grow herself, it will be a wonderful experience for both of you.

FIFTY-TWO

Is it messed up that my girlfriend refuses to stop hanging out with her former lover?

*S*he and I were romantically involved before we were officially dating, but during that time, I found her kissing this other guy (a former lover) while I was in the other room. I confronted her and she apologized, saying that she wanted to be with me. Still, she wouldn't stop hanging out with him.

Even though I don't really care much for labeling things, I eventually decided it was necessary to "make it official" because of the commitment it implies, so I asked her to be my girlfriend, and she said yes. But even now she refuses to stop seeing him.

She often disappears for a day at a time. The last time this happened, when I knew he was at her house, I came over to find that all the pictures of her and I had been moved into a drawer. She said that her cat had *knocked them over, and she needed to find a new place to put them; however, a picture of just her was left unmoved.*

My mother died, and she said she couldn't come to the funeral, because she couldn't find anyone to watch her dog, and she didn't want the other guy to watch her (the dog). But a few days after I returned, I found that her dog is over at this man's house on a "play date."

I could go on and on with examples. But a few days ago, I told her I couldn't stay in this relationship if she was going to keep talking to him. I told her I didn't want her talking to or seeing him anymore. She said I can't control her life, and that it was messed up for me to give her an ultimatum. I need to know if I'm in the wrong.

You're not wrong for this. You're right to have boundaries, as she would be right to have boundaries for you, and to insist that those boundaries be kept. However, this would assume that you were both exclusive, which she never was, and what you did to try to make her treat your relationship exclusively was something you did only because you thought that "making it official" would make her stop seeing him. Therefore, you weren't honest in "making it official" and neither was she.

It's obvious that she wants a relationship with both of you and won't allow you to make her exclusively yours, so the choice is up to you. Is this the relationship you want? You know you can't control her (because there's only one person we can control, and that's ourselves), and if that's what she wants, "making it official" won't stop it. So I ask: what do you want to do? **Do you want to continue this relationship with her, knowing that it will remain a reluctant threesome, or are you willing to let it go?**

We teach people how to treat us—as a priority, or as an option. She doesn't respect what you two have enough to make it exclusive, so are you willing to settle for what she offers you, or do you believe you deserve more? She didn't even respect you enough to come to your mother's funeral. She has said, over and over, how she feels about you. All that's left for you to do is to hear it and decide what you deserve.

If you're willing to settle, complaining about it is useless, and it shows you think little of yourself. If you're not willing to settle, make yourself a priority and find someone who's willing to treat a relationship with you as a priority.

FIFTY-THREE

Anything left to do but move on?

*A*fter talking every day to a woman for six months, we were in a relationship for two and a half months. Then she broke up with me about a month and a half ago because she thought I didn't show enough effort and didn't care for her as much as she cared for me, and she sometimes felt lonely and like only a friend in the relationship.

That hurt to hear, but I took two weeks to think about it and realized that I had been holding back and afraid to be vulnerable due to a past relationship, and just didn't realize it until after she told me when we broke up (she never mentioned it before then).

We've talked a total of three times since the breakup, and I explained to her my insights into my behavior, and that I'm willing to take small steps to see if we can at least be friends, or more if she's comfortable with it. She told me that she appreciated it a lot, it meant so much to her, she believed I was genuine, and that I cared about listening and growing, *which is something she wants out of a partner, but that she's not ready, and needs more time to figure out what she wants.*

The last time we talked was two weeks ago. I haven't reached out since that conversation, and neither has she. But she said other things during that conversation, like "If we get back together, you need to be able to be independent as well", which doesn't really make sense if she thought I wasn't around enough in our relationship. She has also said "I have to make sure this is what I want before possibly spending the rest of my life with you" and "I want to believe that it'll get better, but it's hard to believe it if it wasn't getting better before".

I suggested that we can take small steps and see if they bring us closer together or further apart, but she said she doesn't think she's emotionally ready for that. How does she expect to know if it can get better and if we should try again? What, if anything, can I do?

I've also thought about just reaching out to her to see how she's doing, or saying something like, "If you're not ready by now, I assume you never will be, and I need to close this door so I don't feel like a backup", but is it worth it to do or say any of these things, or would it be better to just let her respond in her own time? Also, what advice do you have for moving on?

What you describe she has said to you sounds contradictory, so I can understand why you're confused, and the fact that it doesn't make sense may mean that you're not seeing the situation as it really is.

She gave signs during the two and a half months that you were together that you didn't notice, and your not noticing those signs were the reason she feels like you don't care as much as she does. In other words, **what you perceived to have happened is different than what she perceived happened, and the things she hoped you'd notice, you didn't.**

She wouldn't've agreed to start the relationship if she didn't want the relationship to work, so she would've tried to salvage the relationship before giving up on it. The fact that you didn't notice the things she was doing to try to save the relationship made her feel like she cared more about it than you did.

You spent two weeks thinking about things, which again showed that you didn't get the signals that she had been trying to give you, and then you concluded that you had been holding back and afraid to be vulnerable due to a past relationship. While there's no reason to doubt that's true, it's not all she wanted you to realize. She wanted you to realize more than what you realized about yourself—she wanted you to realize some things about her, her needs, and her wants, as well. And this may speak to her remark about your needing to be able to be independent. If she believed you behaved as if it was about you and getting your needs met, she doesn't want the pressure of having to be the one meeting all your needs. She wants you to be more independent in the sense that you have friendships outside of her, so that she doesn't have the pressure of needing to be everything that you require.

She wants to let you down easy because she doesn't believe she can have a good relationship with you. She heavily invested herself emotionally, was hurt, and is unwilling to put herself back out there to be hurt again. You can't do anything to make her feel that she should retry this if she's not confident of a good future with you. However fair or unfair it is, the best predictor of future behavior is past behavior.

Is it worth it to reach out to her to say that you need to close the door on the chance of this relationship, so you don't feel like a backup? This question feels like it has some bitterness behind it, so it that's what you feel, it's best you don't ask. But the fact that you pose this question is interesting. Firstly, who makes you feel like a backup? Did she say that you're a backup, or is this something you've created in your own mind? Secondly, she's already closed the door on the chance of a future relationship by her non-responsiveness, so there's really nothing more you need to do in that regard. It would be better to allow her to respond in her own time, if she has anything else to say. In the meantime, you should move on.

What does that mean for you? Take some more time to see where you were selfish in the relationship and why. Whether it was you needing to have your needs met so much that you neglected hers, or whether it was that you weren't healed from your past relationship(s), so you brought your emotional baggage into this relationship, take some more time to reflect on how you can be more emotionally sensitive and available in a future relationship. Heal from your past relationship(s) before pursuing a new one. It's rough emotional work but forgiving both past partners for their mistakes and you for yours goes a long way toward building your emotional health before looking for a romantic relationship with someone else. I wish you the best.

FIFTY-FOUR

I need to vent.

Do you ever just feel like you think you have a best friend, but you start talking about your problems, and then she just starts going on and on about her problems and doesn't even mention yours anymore? Like why am I the one that's always there for her but when it comes to me, it's whatever?

Two things: **we teach people how to treat us**, and there are people who are either unwilling or unable to be true friends to us.

To be best friends with someone, both people must commit equal effort into it. We may consider ourselves best friends with people, but have they shown that they're best friends with us? After all, friendship *is* a two-way street. If others treat us and our needs as unimportant, and we allow it, we're complicit in devaluing ourselves. Anyone who treats you and your needs as insignificant isn't your friend, much less your best friend.

It's possible, though, that your friend doesn't notice she's doing this. Have you ever gently pointed this out to her? I have the impression that you're venting about this because you're afraid to confront her about her behavior. It can be scary to challenge someone about their bad behavior, but if you want her to be a true friend, you must be willing to do so. It's best to talk about it when you're not upset, though. If you wait until you're frustrated, she'll get defensive when you talk about it, and nothing good will be accomplished.

If, after talking about it, she continues to act this way, realize that she's not able to be your best friend, allow yourself to mourn the loss of what you thought you had with her, accept her as she is instead of how you want her to be, and if you still desire someone as a best friend, find someone else emotionally available enough to be your best friend.

FIFTY-FIVE

I was rated a six for my personality by my boyfriend. Why does he stay with me?

I have a boyfriend, and he used to treat me so well. He was the sweetest and would always do nice things for me. But after three months of dating, suddenly he's distancing himself from me. He's always on his phone and asks me strange questions.

Recently he asked me, on a scale of one to ten, how would I rate him? I asked him, are you talking about looks, personality, or both? He said both. I didn't want to answer his question, but he kept on bothering me about it, so I said looks are a nine and personality is a ten. But when I turned the question back on him, he said looks are a seven and personality is a six.

If my personality is so bad, why is he still with me? What does he think of me? Is it likely that that rating will never change, and I'll always be a six to him?

Have you noticed what he's doing on his phone? Is he texting a lot, swiping a lot, or looking at pictures? Do you think he's been talking to someone else? If he's been distancing himself from you, he may be looking for and/or getting what he wants somewhere else.

He asked you a question you didn't want to answer. Though he knew you didn't want to answer it, he didn't respect that, and kept asking until you finally answered. When you answered, you gave answers that seemed kind—maybe *too* kind? **How could *his* personality be a ten when he's distancing himself from you? If his personality was a ten, you wouldn't feel disregarded.** For you to see his personality as a ten would mean that you would feel like you did during the first three months of dating.

I think he asked you that question, over and over, for two reasons. The first reason is because he's insecure. The second reason is because he thought that if he could get you to answer, you'd want to ask him the same questions and would be curious about his answers, which he wanted to give in the first place. He wanted to cause you to feel insecure. Why? For two reasons. The first is because he feels insecure, and misery loves company. The second reason is because insecurity makes you ask the same questions about yourself. It challenges your self-esteem. It makes you want to figure out how to be better *for him*, not for yourself. It makes you want to make *him* happy, rather than *be* happy. It makes you less critical of his bad behavior, and more focused on "improving" yourself to satisfy him. He can continue his bad behavior without being challenged, since you're now focused on what's "wrong" with you.

You ask, "If my personality is so bad, why is he still with me?" There are at least two answers. The first could be that he may believe he's not capable of getting anyone better than you. He may not believe that he's capable of attracting a nine or a ten. The second could be that answering you the way he did gets you to focus on making him happy—to lose yourself, your own identity, in the pursuit of pleasing *him*, in order to increase your rating.

If, after what has been said so far, you still wish him to change his rating of you, the best thing to do is to ask him how you can improve that rating. Listen to his thoughts and decide if they're things you want to do. If you decide they are, do them. If not, be true to yourself and find someone who thinks you're perfect for them just as you are.

FIFTY-SIX

My girlfriend asked for a break after two months of a long-distance relationship. Why do you think she blocked me ten days later?

*M*y girlfriend of two months that I'm in a long-distance rela-tionship with said she needs a break. She said she still loves me but lost some feelings for me and needs time to think, saying I've been a bit dependent, among other small issues. She never communicated about it, but I knew it was something I had to work on.

She doesn't know if she wants to continue the relationship. Then she blocked me ten days into the break that had no end date when we were texting less than once a day.

If this happened to you, why would you assume she blocked you? I want an objective person's perspective on why she'd block me when she agreed *it was okay to text. She says she doesn't really know what she wants, but I think she's just not being honest with herself. Thoughts?*

She's not being completely honest with you because she doesn't want to hurt your feelings. In reality, she knows she doesn't want to continue the relationship, but she's afraid to tell you that. She doesn't want to face disappointing you. Or she's afraid of your reaction.

I would assume she blocked you because **she's no longer interested in speaking with you, but she's afraid to just say so.** I think that even though she agreed that it was okay to text, it was something she didn't want to do. Instead, she felt pressured to agree to it, either because she didn't want to hurt your feelings, or she has trouble saying no to things she doesn't want because she struggles with being a people-pleaser.

I would also assume that she's no longer your girlfriend, the break is actually a break*up*, and you're free to move on.

FIFTY-SEVEN

I recently discovered that the guy I'm casually dating is sending intimate messages to another lady, and I'm confused.

I've been seeing this guy for two months now, and recently discovered he's been texting this other girl intimate messages with love emojis, and they're even planning a trip together. Now, this may not have affected me so much, except for the fact that, at the very start, he expressed the intention to be serious with me.

We had a discussion before this and decided that we would stop seeing other people and focus exclusively on us. To clarify, we weren't boyfriend and girlfriend just yet—just dating exclusively to see if we're a good fit. I agreed to this, and since it was his idea, I didn't think he'd backtrack.

A few weeks ago, I got a feeling something wasn't right, especially because he left the room to pick up a call from another woman. He *usually picks up calls in front of me and doesn't leave the room, so it struck me as odd. I said nothing of it. A few minutes later, this same woman calls again, and he silences his phone. I became curious and confronted him about it. He said it was just his friend and he didn't want to talk to her at the time. I didn't press any further.*

Yesterday, while we were hanging out at my place, he left his phone unattended, and curiosity got the better of me, so I snooped and read their conversation texts. I got so upset, but I haven't confronted him about the matter yet, because I don't know if my emotions are valid.

I feel blindsided because he was the one who said we should date each other exclusively. I'm confused, and I just want to get some advice on the matter.

Part of preparing to love is learning to trust yourself—to trust your feelings, thoughts, and intuition, and to be confident that they're reasonable and valid. You don't trust your thinking about this as being reasonable and valid. What's unreasonable and invalid about the way you think about this situation? He proposed exclusivity; you accepted. Meanwhile, he's not keeping up his end of the proposal.

The fact that he hides his level of involvement with this other woman means that he knows he's doing something he's not supposed to do. If he followed the rules you set together, he would've been honest with you about the other relationship from the beginning.

You could gently confront him about what you saw (after apologizing for invading his privacy, of course) and ask for clarification on how he sees your relationship. It's scary to have a conversation with someone who may tell you something you don't want to hear, but you deserve to know the truth—the truth about where you stand with him, and the truth about where this other woman stands with him.

You could also decide that he lied to you and break off the relationship. Most importantly, though, is to understand why you question the validity of your feelings.

Have you been gaslit? You may be asking yourself what I mean.

Gaslighting is a form of psychological manipulation where a person makes someone question their own sanity, memories, or perception of reality. Has he or anyone else ever made you feel this way? Has he or anyone else denied or dismissed your experiences or emotions? Manipulated facts or twisted information to make you doubt your recollection of events? Blamed you for things that weren't your fault? Invalidated your feelings and experiences, making you feel crazy or overly sensitive?

If you've been gaslit, either by him, others, or both, it may be hard to trust your own perception or feelings. From what you've described here, the things you believe about this situation are valid. If you need to reinforce their validity in your mind, discuss this with a trusted friend or a professional. If you're willing to accept the validity of your thoughts, feelings, and intuition, take any of the actions I've described above.

FIFTY-EIGHT

My boyfriend wants me to quit school and move in with him.

*S*o we've been in a long-distance relationship for over a year or so (we've met before, but live in different countries), and recently he's been talking about me moving in with him and has been pressuring me a lot about it. He's in university, and I'm a high school senior.

At the moment, I'm tempted to actually go through with it, as my living situation is bad, and he's able to pay for tickets, house me, and has money to pay for everything that has to do with me living there, as well as the fact that I'll be much happier, and also have access to therapy and such (which I don't, at the moment).

Though I haven't talked to anyone else about it, I mean I'm fine with it. It would be good to get out of my current living situation, but I'm not sure if it's like a normal thing to do. He also says that he's not sure if he can keep being together with me if I don't visit soon. I don't know what to do. I'm afraid I'll regret it somehow.

You're a high school senior. You've almost completed your education. You've invested about twelve years, and it's almost over. What's his rush? Why can't he wait the few months it'll take for you to get your diploma? What if the relationship ends up not working out—what'll you do then?

You've thought about the pros of making the move, but have you thought about the cons? For instance, you lose your support system when you move to another country. You'll have to learn new customs, you may not be welcomed by his family, he can choose to withhold payment for the things you need if he gets mad at you, and there's so much life that you haven't lived yet. Do you really want to be tied down while you're so young?

It appears he wants you to rely on him, which may make him feel that he has power over you. He may be scared that you won't stay with him if he can't make you dependent on him. If he's not confident you *want* him, he may try to get you to *need* him, so you won't leave him. Is that what you want?

Your fear of regret is a fear of missing out on what you believe could be great, but don't let that fear of missing out cause you to make decisions that you later regret. The fact that you're asking about this decision says that you aren't sure it's the right one. Why pressure yourself to decide to do something you're not confident or comfortable with?

There's a saying I've repeated many times in my life that's helped me in lots of decision-making difficulties: **when in doubt, do without**.

FIFTY-NINE

How do I save my relationship with my dad when his girlfriend keeps coming between us?

I'm 20 and my dad is 50, and we've always had a great relationship. But he's been dating a 23-year-old woman for a year and a half, and ever since she came into his life, everything has turned into a mess—to the point where my dad has even threatened to cut me off.

He just announced that he's about to propose to her and that I must start treating her a little better. I guess she told my dad that I've been rude to her when all I do is not engage with her. I don't care about her inviting me to dinner or to hang out because I just don't like her, and this isn't me being rude.

Somehow, she's omitting the part of the story where she's bossing me around, telling me to do things like she's my mom. This is so frustrating because whatever I say to my dad, I'm the bad guy. She's clearly a gold digger who's using my dad, but he can't see it. Now she's poisoning my relationship with my dad.

At this point, I don't know what to do. I'm forced to be around this woman who's stealing my dad away from me. I'm out of ways of dealing with this situation. My dad doesn't ask me how I feel about this relationship. He clearly doesn't care about my feelings in all of this. I really love my dad, but I fear this new woman is going to cost him our relationship.

What should I do about this situation? Someone please help me figure this out.

What I'm about to tell you will be hard to hear, but necessary for both your happiness and your continued relationship with your father.

All the things that you should do center around one idea—realizing that **you have no control over the decisions your father makes** (except for the control he willingly allows you to have, just as he has no control over the decisions you make, except for the control you willingly allow him to have).

Think of it this way. You believe there's something wrong with your 50-year-old father dating a 23-year-old woman, but what can you do about his decision? You can't *make* him choose otherwise, and he may believe that your rejection of his choice is a rejection of *him*, whereas he feels accepted by his young fiancée. In a battle between choosing someone who you believe accepts you and someone who you believe rejects you, the person who you believe accepts you will always win.

You said she told your dad that you're rude to her when all you do is refuse to engage with her. One can use words to be rude, and one can also use silence to be rude. Since the words we speak only make up 7% of communication, and our nonverbal signals make up 55% of communication, one can argue that it's easier to detect rudeness by refusing to engage with her than to be rude with the words you speak.

Even if you were to say rude words with a rude tone of voice (and the tone of voice makes up 38% of communication), your nonverbal rudeness still outweighs it.

If she's attempting to boss you around, you can simply say no (or just not do it) instead of upsetting yourself by thinking things like, "How *dare* she? I don't know who she thinks she is! She has no right! She's clearly a gold digger who's using my dad!" In other words, it's what you tell yourself about the situation that's causing you to be upset, and it will take changing your thoughts to save your relationship with your dad, despite what they're doing.

You may tell yourself that she's stealing your dad, but that's not actually what's happening. What's happening is that your dad chooses her attitude over yours. You say that he hasn't asked you how you feel about his relationship, but have you shown that you even care about how *he* feels about it? His relationship with his fiancée is not about you; it's about them.

If his fiancée costs you your relationship with your father, it's because you've made that choice. You've made him choose between you and her, and you've made her look like the more attractive option.

So what should you do about this situation? Be as supportive of him as you can, treat his fiancée with dignity and respect, even if you don't respect them because of her age and his decision, and be there for him if his relationship fails, without giving in to the temptation of saying "I told you so" (verbally or nonverbally). There were many times, during your twenty years of life, that your father has had to allow you to make decisions with which he disagreed while treating you with love, dignity, and respect, and he was there to help you pick up the pieces if they turned out as bad as he anticipated. This is your chance to do the same for him.

SIXTY

I'm not in love with my husband anymore. What do I do?

*W*e've only been married for five years. I don't want divorce, because he's still my best friend, and for the most part he's a good father, but he's just really a bad husband.

He sits at the computer playing games all day, then yells that the house isn't clean. We have a four-year-old daughter, and we both have full-time jobs. If he says he's going to help by doing a chore, he leaves it until it can't wait anymore, and I feel I must do it. He's got cats and snakes but does nothing to take care of them. If he puts some dishes in the dishwasher, he claims he's done everything. If I call him out on it, or ask for help, he calls me a liar and says he's the only one that does anything, and it's simply not true.

I have PTSD and try very hard to have a stress-free home. He's allowed to play games—that's not the problem. He's a very anxious person, and I try to give him a peaceful home, but if there's nothing real to worry *about, he looks for things. If he's stressed, he yells, and that's hard for me, because my first instinct is to shut down. I can't do all this alone, but he doesn't acknowledge how much I'm trying to do, which he made apparent this morning when he told me I'm a liar who is the last person in the world with the right to complain.*

What do I do? Like I said, I love him, but I'm just not in love with him anymore. I'm a Christian and can't really justify divorce anyway. My daughter would be devastated. My other friends would stop talking to me. We only have one car, which is under his name. Not that I have any money, because he makes me send him all my money as soon as I get it so he can pay the bills. I'm just tired.

Right now, he has no reason to change. He counts on your unwillingness to demand respect to get away with his bad behaviors. He knows you'll shut down when he yells, do the things he said he would do, and not challenge him on calling you a liar and the last person in the world with the right to complain.

He expects you to work a full-time job *and* take care of the household chores because you've taught him that it's okay to do so. Whenever you complain, he gaslights you, then goes back to his video games. At the risk of repeating myself, I think it would be helpful to explain gaslighting again.

Gaslighting, as I said earlier, is a form of psychological manipulation where a person makes someone question their own sanity, memories, or perception of reality. Has he ever made you feel this way? Has he denied or dismissed your experiences or emotions? Manipulated facts or twisted information to make you doubt your recollection of events? Blamed you for things that weren't your fault? Invalidated your feelings and experiences, making you feel crazy or overly sensitive (as in calling you a liar and the last person in the world with the right to complain)?

He's taking advantage of the fact that you have PTSD and using it against you and for his benefit. He clearly doesn't love you, and he certainly doesn't respect you, because you don't use people you love and respect like he uses you. It's obvious that the things you've suffered cause you to have low self-esteem, and instead of helping you build it, he's taking advantage of it.

You try to give him a peaceful home while he looks for reasons to take away your peace. It's understandable why you're no longer in love with him. In order to be *in* love, you must trust that the person you love has your back, will protect you, is looking out for your best interests, and wants to do things to please you and make your life easier. All the things you do for him, but he doesn't do for you.

How can he be a good father *and* sit at the computer all day playing video games? If you're telling yourself something like "at least he isn't as bad as my father was", **be careful that you don't call a less bad example a good one**. It sounds like there was a lot of turmoil in your home while you were growing up, which would make you value a stress-free home so much that you're willing to give up your right to happiness to have one.

Let's talk about what you can't do if things continue the way they've been before we discuss what you can. You can't change his behavior. You can't cure his anxiety. You can't expect him to pitch in and do his fair share. You can't stop him from yelling. You can't trust him to do what he says. You can't stop him from gaslighting you and pretending everything's your fault. You can't expect him to acknowledge what you do. You can't control how your friends treat you. You can't save any money if you give it all to him.

What *can* you do? Look to the one person you have control over—yourself. Realize that he may be your best friend, but he's an *awful* one, because no good friend treats their friend the way he treats you. Realize that you're experiencing alienation of affection from him, and what you tolerate is what you're teaching your daughter to tolerate from a partner when she's old enough for a romantic relationship. Is that what you want to teach her? Is this the example you want for her?

Stop putting up with his bad behavior, let him know you'll no longer tolerate it, and stick to your guns. If the house isn't clean enough for him, tell him to help. If he says he's going to help by doing a chore, refuse to do it yourself. Tell him that he either takes care of his cats and snakes, or you're going to find a home for them, whether that's with friends or a shelter, and do what you say. Realize that you have no control over what others think of you, and don't let what you think they'll think sway you from your happiness.

I understand the concept of not taking divorce lightly because you're a Christian, but what has been Christian about the life you live with him right now? If you believe your daughter will be devastated if you were to divorce, imagine what she'll be like growing up in a dysfunctional home. If your friends stop talking to you because you're looking for sanity and happiness, they were never really your friends.

Do what's right for you and your daughter.

SIXTY-ONE

How do I break up with a long-distance partner who's currently staying over at my house?

I *'ve been having doubts about my relationship (nearly two years together) for some time now, but due to its very long-distance nature, I was hoping they were caused by me and my girlfriend being apart these last couple of months. Now that she's arrived and is staying for another two weeks, I can see that was not the cause—I'm simply not feeling the way I used to, and I want to break things off. I just feel awful hiding it from her.*

Should I talk with her about it now, or wait until she leaves and do it over the phone? The first choice doesn't make a lot of sense, because she'd still have to stay here for two weeks (can't rebook the plane), and it would make things incredibly awkward, but playing pretend and breaking up over the phone seems cruel.

It sounds like you were having doubts before the two months apart, but talked yourself into believing it had something to do with the long distance. The fact is you knew how you felt before she came back but didn't want to face it within yourself, much less with her.

You could've faced this when you first began to feel this way, but you didn't. You could've faced this when you were apart, but you didn't. You fooled yourself into believing that the problem would just go away, and now you realize it won't.

What can you do now? Neither of your choices is ideal, but between the two of them, the courageous choice is to talk about it face to face. It'll be awkward, but **you must learn to not run from awkward choices**. It would be better to live the truth in the same house for two weeks than to live a lie, and waiting until she leaves to do it over the phone is a cowardly way of doing it. It makes much more sense to be honest.

And you're right—playing pretend and breaking up over the phone *would* be cruel.

SIXTY-TWO

How do I break up with someone who's officially homeless and now lives with me?

*M*y boyfriend lives with me. He was living with his father and stepmother, but the stepmother and my boyfriend didn't get along, so he was kicked out. My boyfriend has a seven-year-old daughter that he sees every other weekend. She stays at my house as well during those times.

We've been together almost a year. He's told me that he will only love his daughter and family (not me). That's all you're supposed to love, in his opinion. I do a lot for him—I pay all his bills, make sure he and his child can eat, and make sure they have a roof over their heads. He doesn't help pay any bills.

I've caught him talking to women on dating apps, Facebook, Snapchat, and text. I don't think I'll ever trust him again. How do I get rid of this leech-seeming man before I lose my mind completely?

You've listed all the reasons you should leave him, so you know that it's something you should do—but you haven't, and that's what I'd like to spend some time discussing, after I've gone over what you've said.

Your boyfriend lives with you, and brings his daughter over to your house, where you provide for both without any assistance from him. He has told you that he doesn't love you, *nor will he*. He hooks up with other women on multiple social media sites.

You said you don't think you'll ever trust him again. When did you trust him in the first place—when he said he'd never love you, when he at no time provided you financial or emotional support, when he leeched off of you, or when he acted on the non-commitment to you that he had from the beginning? If you don't get my point, it's that he never did anything to earn your trust, so trust isn't what you ever felt for him.

In this situation, it's obvious that you allowed yourself to be taken advantage of, used, and treated less than you deserve—the question is why? Why have you put up with this at all, much less for a year?

This problem centers on the fact that you don't believe you deserve to be treated better than he's been treating you, and that's why you ask how to get rid of him. You don't love yourself enough to give yourself better than you've been giving yourself. If you loved yourself, you'd have no problem telling him to go. You wouldn't take another second of being treated that way. People who allow themselves to be treated this way do so because they think it's all they deserve.

Why do they feel this way? It could be because they were told all their lives that they were worthless, undeserving, less than, and there came a point where they believed what they were being told, so that the people that kept them believing this was themselves. If for one minute you believed you deserve better than him, you wouldn't put up with his behaviors, and he wouldn't have even been able to darken your doorstep in the first place.

The fault for him taking advantage of you isn't *his*; it's *yours*. You allow it, and when you believe you deserve better, you'll stop it. "How?" you may ask. **"How do I begin to believe I deserve better than what I've put up with?"**

You begin by asking yourself some honest questions. Who told you that you deserved less, and why? What makes you deserve less than anyone else? Are you less human? No. Have you done more bad things than everyone else? No. Steven Furtick said, "The reason we struggle with insecurity is because we compare our behind-the-scenes with everyone else's highlight reel." You know yourself better than anyone else, but that doesn't mean that you're less than them. You may be focusing on your behind-the-scenes self, with every mistake, while you look at the best of everyone else. It's time for you to begin giving yourself the love and grace you give to others.

In preparing to love yourself, you begin by making a list of all the reasons you deserve to be loved—first, why you deserve to love yourself, and second, why you deserve to be loved by others. You deserve to love yourself in spite of what you think of you or what anyone's said about you. No one's perfect, but you've been willing to give others what you've been unwilling to give yourself.

Tell yourself, "No one's perfect. That includes me. If I'm willing to give love to others, then I deserve love. If I'm willing to be understanding of others, then I need to be able to be understanding of myself. If

I'm willing to excuse others' behaviors, then I need to give myself that same grace. I don't deserve any less than anyone else. If I can love at all, then I can love me. If I can love me, I *will* love me."

Say that over and over, day and night, until it replaces the negative monologue in your brain.

SIXTY-THREE

My boyfriend is jealous of my guy friend.

*M*y boyfriend and I have been dating for eight months. He's incredible, super supportive, the sweetest guy on the planet, and I'm absolutely head over heels in love with him. All my friends absolutely love him, too.

He hasn't shown any controlling or jealous tendencies, encourages me to dress "hot" even though I'm insecure about my body, and lets me hang out with my friends as much as I want, male or female.

Until today.

I have a male friend whom I've known since a year before I met my boyfriend. I developed a huge crush on him (a year and a half ago), confessed this to him, and he turned me down. We became close friends, are still very close friends, and he's in my friend group. It's totally platonic and, although I think he's attractive, I have no feelings for him at all. I told my boyfriend about the crush and confessing and *him turning me down a few months into the relationship, and he didn't have much of a reaction.*

Circumstances led to my ex-crush and my boyfriend not meeting until today. I could instantly tell my boyfriend's vibes were off, and he was being unfriendly to the ex-crush, while usually he's very charming and kind. I could tell he was upset after everyone left and asked him what was wrong. He basically said he didn't feel super comfortable with me being such close friends with someone who I used to have feelings for so recently, that's it a step away from being best friends with an ex, and obviously he couldn't control me, but he was just worried about how it would affect our relationship. I reassured him I had no feelings for the ex-crush at all, and that he's just a friend.

When he left my place, he still seemed not over it, and we were supposed to see each other tomorrow and this weekend, but he just texted me asking if he could just do his own thing this weekend and see me Sunday.

What's going on here? How can I reassure him?

Contrary to the opinion of some, there are things you should never share with your partner, because they could prove too hard for your partner to handle. Think of it this way: **before sharing something regarding your past with your partner, ask yourself what benefit it'll have for your relationship**. If the answer is none, why share it? But if it helps your partner understand why you react in a way that hurts the relationship, share it. It'll help your partner understand the motivation behind your actions, help them to not take it personally, and help give them patience to stick with the relationship while you work to deal with it.

Sometimes, we think that sharing all the things that happened in our past is simply being honest, even when it's not necessary. Giving details about things that happened before you started a relationship with someone isn't always done just to be honest, though—sometimes, it's simply to ease feelings of guilt. Perhaps you subconsciously think it's wrong to have a friendship with someone you once had romantic feelings for. If you feel this way, it's up to you to ask yourself if you really have anything to feel guilty about. If you can't find a reason you should feel guilty, it's up to you to work with your feelings until they change (unless your partner's mature enough to help you overcome your guilty feelings, which is incredibly rare).

When you told your boyfriend about your other friend, he didn't want to tell you how he felt in the beginning, which is why he didn't show much of a reaction when you first told him. I'm sure he didn't bring it up since then, either, because he didn't want to face something so hurtful for him. However, when he came face-to-face with the friend, he could no longer avoid his feelings about him, which you saw. He wonders if the fact that you told him means that you still have feelings for your male friend, despite you saying you don't.

Since you can't put that genie back in the bottle, you're left with allowing him space to figure this out for himself (which he's asked for with wanting to spend the weekend without you), while you make sure he knows, by your actions, that he's the only man you love. You can't have it both ways—overshare and expect things to be like they were before—however, it's possible that, once he deals with his feelings, your relationship will be deeper than before. On the other hand, it's possible that he won't be able to deal with his feelings about this, and you may lose him.

SIXTY-FOUR

My ex reached out after his current girlfriend broke up with him.

L *ooking for some advice.*

My ex broke up with me last year, and he immediately got into a relationship with the person he told me not to worry about. I was devastated.

However, he reached out to me this week and revealed that she had just broken up with him. We've chatted a few times since we broke up, but this is the first time he's reached out. They were together for ten months.

He's chatting with me like the last ten months didn't happen, and reminiscing about things him and I did together. Am I a fool for talking to him? What do I do? What's going on in his head? Thanks!

From the things you describe, I assume that you want a romantic relationship with him, and have wanted it since the breakup, but now that it's beginning to sound to you like he might want that same relationship with you, you wonder if it's a good idea. Let's examine this further.

It's highly likely that your ex started the relationship with the person who just broke up with him before he broke up with you, you suspected it, confronted him about it, and he told you not to worry about her. In other words, at some level he was cheating on you. You were devastated, but this didn't stop you from wanting him back.

You mentioned that it was always you reaching out to him before he reached out to you this time. This shows that you wanted to stay in touch with someone who devastated you, who trampled on your trust, and who violated your heart. Why? Because you hoped he'd change his mind and come back to you.

He reached out to you. He told you she broke up with him. He reminisced about the times you had with him before the two of you broke up. He acted like he never devastated you.

Are you a fool for talking to him? What's the difference between talking to him the times you reached out to him and talking to him when he reached out to you? If those times weren't foolish, why is this time foolish? Or put another way: if this time's foolish, those times were, too.

Do you imagine he reached out to you to get back together? How will you know? There's only one way: ask him. **If you want to know what's going on in his head, ask.** Ask him if he wants to get back together.

What do you do? Do you believe that won't leave you again? If it were me, I wouldn't entertain the thought of getting together again. If he didn't respect you enough to be honest before, what would have changed? But if you decide to try a romantic relationship with him again (assuming that's what he wants), I recommend you insist that it be a celibate one for a certain amount of time, to see if it's really you he wants, or just sex.

Steve Harvey, in his book *Act Like a Lady, Think Like a Man*, recommends 90 days of celibacy at the start of a romantic relationship, and I think that would be a good idea in this situation. If he shows that he loves you and wants the relationship after being celibate 90 days, there's a good possibility he's there to stay. If not, you'll have your answer.

SIXTY-FIVE

My boyfriend didn't get me anything for Valentines Day and then asked me about an open relationship.

I had mentioned and asked him to plan something a week ago. I've also mentioned to him multiple times in the four years that we've been together that he doesn't ever plan anything for my birthday, holidays, doesn't get me gifts, etc., and how that's something that's special and important to me.

Anyway, I got him flowers and treats and snacks, and he promised he'd make it up to me, so I said alright, let's see what he does.

Then this morning he texted me while still in bed and I'm taking care of the kids: "Can I ask you a hypothetical question? Is there any scenario where you'd consider being in an open relationship?"

He's asked this before, and my answer is always no. And I've told him repeatedly that if we are going to have a better sexual relationship (stale *at this point), he* **must** *put more effort into our relationship. He does the bare minimum on a good day. We constantly fight about chores, the kids, who gets more free time, sex, bad communication, etc., and I've asked for more for years.*

I'm in complete and utter shock right now that he thought this was the time to ask me that question. After making me feel unimportant and like he can't put one second of effort into making me happy or showing he loves me.

What would you suggest doing in this scenario?

He's not interested in making you happy. His own happiness and comfort are more important to him. You do things that you hope will make him happy, and that you'd like done for you. He believes he deserves the things he receives but doesn't want to give. Furthermore, since you've told him the things that make you happy, he's told you what'll make him happy, as if he'll be more thoughtful if you'll agree to an open relationship.

The question is: what will you do about it? Has anything else you've done up to this point worked? No. Einstein said insanity is doing the same thing over and over while expecting different results. This isn't to say you were wrong by being thoughtful to him and hoping for him to be thoughtful in return. It's simply to get you to ask yourself, **"Why do I keep doing the same things, never getting the outcome I want, but somehow think they'll eventually work?"** If you find yourself on a hamster wheel, working hard but going nowhere, what do you do? You get off.

You hope that you mean more to him than you do, and you work hard to try to mean more to him, but it doesn't work. The constant fighting to be heard, to be seen, to be regarded, to be respected, and to be valued has produced nothing.

Do you deserve more from him? Absolutely. Is it likely that you'll get what you deserve from him? No. Can you make him treat you better? Absolutely not. He must want to, and he doesn't. So now the question falls on you: how will you get the love you deserve? Not from him. So why do you stay? For the kids?

The kids see the dysfunction in your relationship, and that does them more harm than if you were no longer together. Staying together for the sake of the children doesn't do them, or you, any favors.

Let him know that under no circumstance will you consider an open relationship. Acknowledge the love you deserve to both you and him and give him an ultimatum. Realize, though, that when you do, you must do what you said you would if he doesn't give up this idea and love you more thoughtfully. If you don't, he'll know that he can get away with the way he treats you, because you'll eventually give up trying to get him to treat you better, and you won't insist on the love you're worthy of. Ultimately, you must love yourself enough to stop settling for less than you deserve.

SIXTY-SIX

A girl in my friend group won't stop hitting on my boyfriend.

*T*here's this girl in my friend group who keeps hitting on my boyfriend every time we hang out.

The main issue is this: I'm super introverted and going out takes a lot out of me. Whenever she's there, I simply can't enjoy myself, as she makes me feel deeply unsettled. Not only does she hit on my boyfriend (touching his leg, his arm, responding to every comment he makes even if there's ten of us hanging out), but she also makes sure to belittle me every chance she gets (like mentioning a personal health issue I had in the past, that she overheard from another friend, in front of everyone).

My boyfriend and I have talked about this situation, and he agrees with me. He makes a conscious effort to not engage with her, but she's obnoxious to the point where not responding to her would stand out as rude. We have a super healthy and loving relationship. It's external issues like this one that we don't know how to handle, as we both don't like awkward situations. Help! What do I do?

The easy answer is to no longer have her be a part of your friend group and let her know that you no longer want to hang out with her because it makes you uncomfortable, but if you're concerned about her thinking badly of you as a result, you may not want to do this. Let me offer some reasons why you may consider this, though.

First, she has no respect for you, and friendship requires respect. She's not your friend if she doesn't respect you—therefore, she shouldn't be in your friend group. In other words, at the risk of stating the obvious, friend groups should consist of friends.

Second, not only does she hit on your boyfriend—she belittles *you*. It sounds like she's jealous of you and wants to take your boyfriend in hopes of having the relationship with him that you do. **Her actions are the classic example of jealousy as the cousin of greed.** If she were your friend, she'd be happy for you, not jealous of you.

Third, your boyfriend isn't the one being rude by not responding to her advances—she's being rude by hitting on him, especially in front of you (which goes back to her lack of respect for you). In learning to love yourself, you must consider your feelings before considering hers, not treating her feelings as more important than yours, or your feelings as the doormat for her to walk all over. If your boyfriend comes off as rude to her because he doesn't acknowledge her advances, so be it. Her opinion of either of you is less important than your opinion of the situation.

Of course, the ideal thing would be for you and your boyfriend to sit her down and tell her how her behavior makes you feel. If you're able to do that and she apologizes and acts more like a friend, you'll finally have her as a true in friend. If you're unable to do this, though, the next best thing would be to no longer invite her to do friend group things with the two of you. Hopefully, when she asks why, you'll be able to tell her, but if you're not there yet, at least you've eliminated that stress from your life.

SIXTY-SEVEN

My girlfriend is asexual, and I wonder if I'm sacrificing my own needs out of fear of not finding another amazing person like her.

We've been together for six years this month, and she's my best friend. I couldn't imagine losing her.

Early in the relationship, she realized that sex made her uncomfortable. I was inexperienced at that time, so I honestly didn't know if that would be an issue for me.

Now we're six years in, and I can't say that it's a constant *weight on my mind, but I've started wondering if I'm pushing my own needs/wants down out of fear of not finding anyone else. I don't resent her in any way for the lack of sex.*

It just feels like a small thing to end a good relationship over. Even though I know it isn't a small thing.

How do I decide whether it's a big enough issue to end this relation-ship?

You decide if it's a big enough issue by asking yourself if, given the opportunity, you would feel justified in cheating on her because she's not intimate with you.

If you received a message from an ex-girlfriend saying that she's been thinking about you and wants to know if you're interested in hooking up, how do you think you'd respond?

Do other women flirt with you? If so, how do you respond? Do you simply acknowledge their attention and walk away, or do you fantasize about being sexual with them? If another woman touched you in order to arouse you, would you let it continue, or would you stop it and say that you're already in a committed relationship?

You're right—sex (or the lack thereof) is no small thing. **If it's important to you, it's important.** Here are some things for you to consider:

What are your needs, desires, and long-term goals in this relation-ship? How important is sexual intimacy to you, and do you believe you can feel fulfilled in the relationship without it?

Have you had an open and honest conversation with your girlfriend asking why she's uncomfortable with sex? Her reasons are important and, depending on the reasons, would be handled in different ways. There's a huge difference, for instance, between her being uncomfort-able because of trauma caused by being assaulted by someone in her past versus being uncomfortable because it physically hurts her (e.g., dyspareunia, vaginismus), and the treatments would be different.

Are there ways to find a middle ground or compromise that respect both your sexual needs and your girlfriend's lack of sexual fulfillment?

Would she be willing to seek professional guidance on overcoming being uncomfortable with it, whether through a doctor or a therapist?

After you have this conversation, you'll be able to determine if maintaining this relationship is right for you, or if it'd be better to simply remain good friends.

SIXTY-EIGHT

My boyfriend is mad that I got an apartment.

I've been dating my boyfriend for a little under a year. I'm currently in the process of moving as my landlord gave me notice to move from my current apartment, stating that his son wants to move in. My boyfriend has also been in the process of apartment hunting (we agreed it was a little sudden to move together and would rather it be gradual).

I found a place that I signed for yesterday. My 37-year-old boyfriend now says that he doesn't want to date anymore until he finds his own place, because it makes him feel inadequate (he lives with his brother, sister-law, and their children).

I feel like it's BS because he could find an apartment if he took some initiative. My property owner also divulged that my boyfriend's yelling and stuff were factors in why he evicted me, because I had been fine for years beforehand.

I'm not sure how to feel about this situation. Should I just say screw it and give up on him?

You're right—your boyfriend could've gotten an apartment for himself if he really wanted to. The fact that he didn't is telling.

It's good that your boyfriend says he doesn't want to date anyone until he gets his own place because it makes him feel inadequate. When I said that the fact that he doesn't have his own apartment is telling, this is what I meant—he may be beginning to realize that he's not ready for a relationship. He may realize that he needs to work on himself before he's ready to share his life with someone else.

You said that one of the reasons you had to move was because of your boyfriend's yelling. Assuming this refers to him yelling at you, it's possible that he wasn't happy in the relationship and wanted to end it anyway. He may be using the situation with the apartment to do something he already wanted to do. Of course, this assumes that he isn't mad about *you* getting an apartment—rather, he may be mad about you putting pressure on *him* to get one.

His brother and sister-in-law also feed his feeling of inadequacy by not demanding he live on his own. This is called enabling.

What else do enablers do to allow people to continue self-sabotaging behaviors?

They overlook or downplay the negative results of the actions of the people they enable. They continuously come to the aid of the people they enable, preventing them from facing the consequences of their behavior. They make excuses for them by justifying or rationalizing their actions to others. They put the needs of the people they enable before their own, even when it's damaging to them. They give them money to sustain their harmful habits. They try to hide or protect them from the consequences of their behavior. They refuse to acknowledge the seriousness of their actions or the impact of the enabled person's behaviors on others. They shift responsibility for the actions of the people they enable by blaming others. They don't hold the people they enable responsible for their actions. And enablers keep doing it instead of trying to get the enabled to change.

He's not ready for the relationship with you, but that's no reason to say screw it and give up on him. In other words, anger over the situation shouldn't motivate your response. If you love him, accept that he's not ready for the relationship with you because of things he needs to work on in himself, and let that motivate your response. While it will still mean that you no longer have a romantic relationship, it may allow you to forgive him and maintain some level of friendship. Most of all, **be careful how you exit a relationship, because it'll determine how you'll enter the next one**.

SIXTY-NINE

My husband has money for golf, but never for romance or me.

I never thought I would make excuses for a man like this, but I'm newly postpartum and don't want to see the writing on the wall. Last year, my husband skipped celebrating our ten-year wedding anniversary after I told him it was important to me. No gift, no celebration—nothing. I don't even remember what we did that day. His reasoning was that we didn't have enough money to do anything nice. He has the same reason for not getting birthday gifts, push presents (presents given to the mother by the partner or family to mark the occasion of giving birth to a child)—anything. He even complains about grocery store makeup or budget-tier clothes for me and the kids. It's not like he communicates that he appreciates me in other ways, though.

Now he wants to join an expensive country club and tells me the (thousands of dollars) initiation fee isn't a concern because he's been secretly saving for it. He says it's for the family, and sure, the kids might *use it, but it's mainly so he can golf and pretend to be successful on weekends.*

These are grounds for divorce, right? I feel like there's no way to point it out to him because he'll then retroactively get me whatever gifts I want once he sees it as a barrier to club entry. I feel like he's telling me very clearly what our marriage is worth to him, and it's not much. It sucks when I've just had our third baby. On top of not feeling very confident, I'm not interested in throwing our kids' lives into chaos.

Thanks for your perspective on this.

Have you tried communicating what this means to you and how devastating his decisions have been for you, or do you believe you shouldn't have to tell him because he should know how this makes you feel?

If he retroactively gets you gifts because of having this conversation with him, it shows that he took the wrong thing away from the conversation you had with him about it, or it may show that you focused on the wrong thing when you talked with him about it. A conversation that contains, "you can't afford gifts for me but you can seem to afford an expensive country club initiation fee" is different from one that says, "when you say you can't afford to celebrate our ten-year wedding anniversary, or to give me birthday gifts, push gifts, or even budget-tier clothes for the kids and I, but you can afford an expensive country club initiation fee, it makes me feel worthless, unimportant, and that our marriage isn't worth much to you." The first is accusatory and asks for tangible solutions, while the second asks him to examine his heart and, if the happiness of his family is more important to him than impressing others, to prove it—first, by being sorry, and second, by changing his priorities.

Divorce is an option, but there are lots of other options between where you are and that, like having conversations about your feelings (it may take more than one), including that you feel unappreciated in other ways, as well.

If he'll retroactively buy you gifts only to get to have his country club membership, and he wants the membership to pretend to be successful, he may only be interested in status, which may include the façade of a happy marriage and family. Figure out if status is the most important thing to him, and if it is, determine if you're okay with being less important than status. If you're not okay with it, gently give him the ultimatum of choosing to make his family the most important thing, with consequences if he doesn't, and be ready to follow up on those consequences if he chooses status over you.

Relearning to love yourself results in knowing your worth and not settling for less than what you deserve. Set clear boundaries with him regarding what you will and won't tolerate. Communicate your needs and expectations, and if you're afraid to walk away from this relationship if he doesn't meet them, you may need to feel the fear and do it anyway. Surround yourself with supportive people who uplift you and remember that it's okay to prioritize your own happiness and well-being.

SEVENTY

My girlfriend made secret plans with her guy coworker.

My girlfriend and I have been having problems because she's getting closer to her guy coworker, and she thinks there's nothing wrong with keeping up with some guy from work. They've hung out in a group together, and she texts him and he checks up on her. Everyone at her job knows that she's with me, but every time he texts her, she says it's about work.

I recently found out that she paid to go to an event with this guy and she removed the messages about planning it together. This all looks bad, and I'm about ready to just let her go, because she's hiding things from me and making plans to hang out with this dude behind my back. Why stop it?

I think I should break up with her and focus on myself. Help, please.

It's obvious that your girlfriend believes that what she's doing is right and that she's going to do it regardless of how you feel about it.

She hid the plans she was making with her friend from you not because she believed it was wrong, but she didn't want to have to deal with your response if you found out she made those plans.

It's also obvious that she knows how you feel about it, and it doesn't matter to her, except for sneaking to do what she wants because she doesn't want to have to face your reaction.

She's made her position on the matter clear. The question is this: will you do the same?

This isn't about figuring out who's the most stubborn. It's not about winning or losing. It isn't a contest. No one has to play chicken. Both you and she have the right to make your choices and deal with the consequences, and that doesn't have to be thought of as a bad thing. Consequences themselves are neither good nor bad—they just *are*.

She made a choice—it was to maintain a friendship that makes you uncomfortable. The fact that you're uncomfortable isn't enough for her to cut off the friendship. Your only option in this case (as in every circumstance) is to stop trying to control that over which you have no control (her) and to focus on what you can control (you).

What will you do? Is it okay that she does this? If it isn't, why stay miserable in the relationship? **You can be miserable all by yourself. Why be with someone with whom you feel miserable?**

You suggested that you should focus on yourself, which is another way of saying you want to deal with whatever's going on in you that allowed you to remain with someone who considers your needs so little. I agree with you.

SEVENTY-ONE

I'm hurt by my husband's porn search results.

*M*y husband and I have been together for seven years and have been married for three years. His porn search has always bothered me, but I made myself believe it was normal, even though it hurt my feelings back then, too.

His porn history consists of things like teen, super petite, tiny. All the girls are 18-23 years old and super tiny, short, and skinny.

I'm the opposite of his searches—super busty and curvy. I've gained some weight since pregnancy and during a severe depression relapse. I've lost 40 pounds now, but I still have a lot more to lose. And now I'm almost 28 years old. His search history is girls about 10 years younger than me and with a weight of around 95 pounds, and he only watches POVs so to me it's like he imagines he's having sex with them.

I allow him privacy. I've only looked a handful of times in seven years, and that's only when I have a bad feeling. He cheated on me once. It was online, and he sent nudes and was sexting an 18-year-old girl about *three months into our marriage. I almost left, and he said he messed up. I only stayed since it wasn't physical, and I caught him early—about a week into him doing it.*

Am I wrong for feeling hurt? Am I crazy? I'm trying to work on myself. I've told him in the past how it hurts, but it's never changed his actions. He still saves the videos, and it all feels wrong and hurts.

Any advice or opinions?

Thoughts can be wrong, but feelings can't. Let me explain.

Feelings are indicators of conscious thoughts, subconscious thoughts, or both. Feelings are just alerts that ask you to examine their source (the thinking behind the feeling) more deeply. The hurt asks, "What are you thinking that cause me?"

Do you believe that his actions are a direct reflection of your lack of worth, and does this cause you to feel inadequate or unworthy? Do you think that his actions say that you're not good enough, that you're not young enough, and that you're not skinny enough?

How do you become convinced that you're worthwhile? Who convinces you? Is it him, or is it you? You may be saying, "I know it's supposed to be me, but that's easier said than done." You know what? You're right—it *is* easier said than done—but that doesn't mean it *shouldn't* be done because it's not easy!

It's admirable that you've been trying to work on yourself, but what exactly about yourself have you been trying to work on? Your appearance only? Or both your appearance and your perception of yourself? The appearance is much easier to work on than self-perception, but the self-perception is more needful and produces more permanent results.

Apparently, he knows how you feel about his porn searches, but he does it anyway. You do your best to allow him autonomy, only investigating further when your intuition tells you to. A woman's intuition is powerful, and not to be taken lightly. If you have a bad feeling, there's a good possibility that there's a reason for it. It doesn't necessarily mean that he's cheating, but whether he is or not may depend on your definition of cheating. For some, it takes engaging in physical sex for them to consider it cheating. For others, it's sending nudes to someone else, or sexting, or emotional cheating, or even watching porn.

Do you believe he's cheating in his imagination when he watches porn? If you do, it's not surprising that it hurts you. Does he push the boundary, knowing that you won't leave him if it doesn't become physical, or even limit himself to sexting? You may be telling yourself, "I should be enough for him, but apparently, I'm not." That belief alone can cause so much anguish, pain, and hurt.

As I see it, you have two choices. The first choice is to no longer tolerate his watching porn, telling him so, stating the consequences if he does, and following through with those consequences if you catch him doing it. If this is your choice, you must be ready to carry out the consequences you gave, because if you don't, he'll know you're just talking with no intention of doing what you said you'd do.

The second choice is to figure out how to live with him watching porn without taking it personally. If this is your choice, here's how to minimize your pain.

First, realize that, even though he occasionally fantasizes about being with someone else, he still comes home to you. It's not ideal—you want to be not only his wife, but his fantasy, and you don't want to share the spot of being his fantasy with anyone else. But there's what you want, and then there's the truth. No relationship is ideal—there are things we wish the other person would do, say, and be—and the sooner we accept that they won't be, say, or do everything we imagined they would, but that we love them anyway, the sooner we get off the hamster wheel of false and crushing expectations.

Second, understand that it's what you tell yourself that causes you pain. For instance, if you're telling yourself, "He sees how saving those videos hurts me. If he loved me, he would stop!" or "I should be enough for him", these thoughts cause no end of pain. If you change the thoughts, however, you change the pain. For instance, instead of saying, "If he loved me, he would stop!" understand the difference between men and women. For many women, love and sex are connected, and it's unimaginable to have one without the other. This isn't the case for most men, and the perfect example for this is how men feel during and after an argument.

An argument can leave a woman feeling unloved and unappreciated. The last thing on her mind at that point is sex. However, men compartmentalize, so that an argument is an argument, sex is sex, and the two don't have to have anything to do with one another. Men have no problem having sex after an unresolved argument. The issue will still be there afterwards, men tell themselves—why should that have anything to do with sex?

And instead of telling yourself, "I should be enough," follow this general rule when thinking the word should—change it to "it would be nice if", as in "It would be nice if I was enough." That's the truth without creating a firm rule that causes you more pain. After all, it's easy enough to defeat the idea that you should be enough by asking the question, "Why should you?" Even if you say, "Because I'm his wife!" that still begs the question, "What rule is there that mandates that a wife should be enough? Where is it written? Is it a commandment?" Even from a biblical viewpoint (if that's your worldview and you want to pursue the idea of a commandment), the same people who were told not to covet (desire) their neighbor's wives were allowed to have more than one wife.

From this, you can see that you're creating an absolute that is not only untrue but is the author of your pain. If you're not enough, mandating that you should be won't make you enough. It's better to accept the reality of what is than to distress over the fantasy of what you wish would be. Then you are no longer powerless, but can take whatever actions you need to, whether it's to learn to love yourself, to accept the reality of what is, to leave, or any combination of the three.

SEVENTY-TWO

My current partner thinks it's weird that me and the father of my child are on good terms.

*S*o my ex and I share a toddler. My current partner thinks it's weird that we talk on the phone to give updates about the kid and that I send him photos of fun things she does.

My ex invited me and my partner to the beach, and my current partner thinks it's weird and doesn't want me to go. I grew up in a house where my parents were divorced but still friends and still did stuff together. It seems normal to me. It's not like my current partner isn't invited, which would be weird for sure.

Is it so weird to do things as a "family" for the sake of the kid?

The question isn't really "is it weird" as in a common measure of weirdness that's the same no matter who the two people are, but "is it weird to him, and if so, why?"

Obviously, **there's no universal standard of weirdness**. Some things eaten in one country, for instance, can be considered weird in another. Customs in one country are sometimes considered weird in another country. There's nothing done universally that there's not at least one person who thinks it's weird.

So let's answer the questions, "is it weird to him, and if so, why?" The answer to the first part is obviously yes, because he told you so. As to why, I'm pretty confident that he's not used to seeing exes get along as well as you and your ex does. He probably hasn't seen any relationships that didn't end with the two people despising each other, so your situation is weird *to him*. Not wrong, not right—just *weird*.

You, on the other hand, have parents who were divorced but were still friends and did stuff together, so this is normal for you. Understand that it has nothing to do with whether it's weird, and everything to do with the differences between your past experiences.

As to your question, "Is it so weird to do things as a 'family' for the sake of the kid?" I ask instead, "Is it healthy for a child to see his parents get along, not hate on each other, love the child in front of each other, and know that these parents can get along and still be friends even when the mom and dad are with someone else, and that person (or those persons) is (or are) there?" There can only be one answer: yes!!

SEVENTY-THREE

My wife is texting another guy that is "just a friend" but they're talking about meeting up.

*M*y wife has a habit of making friends off the internet, especially guys. It's been a big deal in the past, but we concluded that I didn't mind as long as it stayed on the app and maybe go to Snapchat, but absolutely no giving out personal numbers.

Well recently she ended up sharing her number and started talking to another guy. Her reasoning was "he doesn't have any social media". I told her I didn't like it. I became the bad guy, with her saying stuff like she can't talk to anyone. I called her out on it as emotionally cheating. That turned into me reading into things. Whatever.

I don't like it and she pushed me away because of it. She talks to this person constantly. This morning, I checked her phone, and they were talking about meeting up. I don't want to admit that I checked it, but I *was curious. If I have nothing to worry about, it shouldn't be a big deal, right? Well, now I don't know how to bring it up without it becoming a huge issue.*

That's where I need advice. What's the best way to handle this? I trust her, but she did break one stipulation that I had. Am I being overbearing and stupid about this?

It concerns me that you say, "We concluded that I didn't mind..." That phrasing sounds like you were manipulated, as opposed to "*I* concluded that I didn't mind". The fact that you think you're being "overbearing and stupid" means you don't trust your own ability to reason. She obviously knows this and uses it to do what she wants while lying about it.

She said she shared her number with a guy because "he doesn't have any social media". If she was only supposed to meet people using apps, how did she meet a guy who has no social media? There's obviously a lie (or lies) in here, and you were right to call her out on it (or them).

Why do you trust her when she has clearly done something she agreed not to do? Perhaps you trust her because you think you're supposed to, not because she's been trustworthy. This is another example of you not trusting yourself and your ability to correctly figure out what's going on here. The reason is because you're being gaslit.

The fact that she made you out to be the bad guy is a classic example of gaslighting. I'm going to give you some other examples and ask yourself if any of these have ever happened:

Has she ever denied that she said or did something, even though you clearly remember it happening?

Has she ever downplayed your feelings or experiences, making you feel like your concerns are unimportant or exaggerated?

Has she ever blamed you for her actions, making you question whether you're responsible for the situation?

Has she ever withheld information to manipulate your perception of events or keep you in the dark?

Has she ever contradicted what you know to be true, making you doubt your memory or understanding of things?

Has she ever accused you of behaviors or thoughts she was actually engaging in, causing you to question your own intentions?

Has she ever twisted facts or manipulated situations to make it seem like you're the one who's mistaken?

If any of these are true, you've been gaslit.

Here's what you do: **learn to love yourself enough to trust your instincts.** Get professional support with this if you need to. Document instances where you feel you're being gaslit, and gain and maintain a sense of self-confidence. Address her manipulative behaviors, and don't be put off when she tries her usual gaslighting tactics. Most of all, love yourself enough to prefer being miserable without her to being miserable with her, if necessary. After all, you can be miserable all by yourself—you don't need her to make you miserable.

SEVENTY-FOUR

My partner always tells me that other women are prettier or better looking than me whenever we get into arguments.

*H*e always does this. He's notorious for looking at other women. Whenever I catch him staring, I call him out on it and we end up arguing about it. He's the type that says really foul things when he's upset. He always ends up saying they look better than me, then later says he didn't mean it, he regrets it, etc., but he does this **every time**. One time he even said my sister was prettier than me.

It really messes with my self-esteem. I'm now starting to question why he's even with me if every woman looks better than I do. Do I take his word that he's just saying things out of anger, or should I believe that, deep down inside, he truly thinks I'm unattractive, which is why he continues to bring it up?

He's pushing the one button he knows will always work and will get you to stop arguing with him, not caring about the devastation and heartache it causes you. He does what it takes to continue to do what he wants to do, which is disrespecting you by ogling women in front of you while keeping you from responding appropriately to it.

Is it fair? No. Is it nice? No. Is it loving? Absolutely not. But if you allow him to keep doing it, you teach him that it's okay to continue treating you this way. My questions to you are these: are you okay with him doing it, and if not, what are you going to do about it?

I think it's safe to assume that you're not okay with him doing this, and you shouldn't be. If he actually thought you were unattractive, it wouldn't take him getting angry to tell you, and if you were undesirable, he wouldn't continue to be with you. Why, then, does he keep bringing this up? He may be projecting his feelings about himself onto you, finding his own lack of self-esteem too painful to face.

Projection is a defense mechanism in which someone attributes their own undesirable thoughts, feelings, or behaviors onto another person. He very likely considers himself unattractive and undesirable, and instead of acknowledging that he feels that way about himself, he accuses you of them. Have you heard the saying, "Misery loves company"? It may be that he's miserable and wants to drag you down into his self-misery by ripping away at your self-esteem.

Even if what he says is true, and he only say these things out of anger, you deserve to be treated better than he treats you. **You deserve to be loved, admired, and be with someone who, at the end of the day, only has eyes for you.**

While it's common to admire the beauty of others, it's not okay to point out to our significant other things that mess with their self-esteem. It's also not okay to be disrespectful to our significant other when we do it. And it's absolutely not okay to destroy others with our words just because we're angry. But is the standard you set for yourself really going to boil down to whether he's saying those things out of anger, or that he actually finds you unattractive? Is it okay for him to find you attractive if he only says you're unattractive out of anger? Hopefully the answer to these questions is no, and you learn to love yourself enough to insist that you're treated with the love, respect, and admiration you deserve.

SEVENTY-FIVE

My boyfriend really embarrassed me, and it's making me reconsider our relationship.

*E*arlier today, my boyfriend and I went to an amusement park in our city that has high security. My boyfriend carries a knife for protection as well as to help him out at work and forgot to leave it in his car.

We get to the gate, and they have metal detectors, cops everywhere, and people checking bags like it's an airport. There has been a history of violent fights because it draws such large crowds, so they check people like crazy before entry.

The security guard scans my boyfriend with a metal detector and my boyfriend tells him he carries a knife for work. Then the security guard said, "nah, you guys can't enter with that." That's when this other female security guard came up to us doing the absolute most, saying things like *"you gotta go", "where did you park?", and "we've got cameras—we'll be watching you", as if my boyfriend was about to stab someone right then and there. My boyfriend decides to tell the lady off as we turn around to leave.*

As we keep walking, the lady gets closer to the fence to watch us and keeps telling us there's cameras, and my boyfriend was like, "f*** off don't f***ing talk to me", gives her the finger, and makes a scene. I then told him, "Babe, chill out—we're going anyway so let's not get into more s***", then he goes off on me saying, "stop being a p****—what are they gonna do?"

*I was angry and embarrassed. I try to calm down so he and I don't get tackled by a cop or arrested over nothing (especially since we're both people of color), and he decides to turn around and tell **me** off?*

He then tries to hug me as we're walking back to his car saying, "I'm sorry, babe," but I was too annoyed. I didn't speak to him at all for the whole ride back and I haven't texted him the whole day.

Honestly, the situation really pissed me off. Is it wrong that I'm reconsidering whether I want to be with him anymore? I really didn't like the way he conducted himself, and I feel like it's changed the way I see him.

There was a lot going on and you experienced various levels of emotions, such as ones you described (anger, embarrassment) and ones you didn't (fear for your life, stunned). As a fellow person of color, I understand that we can't afford the luxury of always expressing everything we think, understanding that we take our own lives in our hands in ways others don't. Nor could they understand.

Your boyfriend, however, seemed to throw all caution to the wind, and not only endanger himself with his regretful behavior, but also endanger you, who alone looked past the incident to its possible consequences. Besides that, you expected better self-control from him, and you certainly didn't expect him to turn on you for something you had nothing to do with creating. And all this is besides the fact that it sounds like he knew he had the knife on him before he got scanned and attempted to carry it into the amusement park anyway.

In your mind, his cavalier attitude could've gotten you arrested or killed. Then, while you try to de-escalate the situation, he goads you because you didn't join him in his actions, though you see it as him telling you off. He thought he was right to say what he said to the female security guard and didn't understand why you didn't feel the same way. He looked at the incident from an immature perspective, while you looked at it from a mature one.

Is it wrong that you're reconsidering whether to stay with him? It's never *wrong* to consider it, or even reconsider it, as you're never bound to remain in a situation where you don't feel safe. Perhaps a better question would be: should you *continue* a relationship with him?

An important thing to consider is this: **the length of a relationship doesn't guarantee its quality.** In fact, people who behave badly don't usually behave better when you agree to stay in it for the long haul; they tend to behave worse. A common belief among many who are considering marriage is that they can overlook bad behavior before marriage because it'll get better once they're married. But that's hardly ever the case. People trying to get a greater commitment from you will act right to keep you from denying them that commitment, then once they have it, they feel the pressure's off, so they have no more reason to act right.

What do you do from here? I suggest you let him know that you won't tolerate this behavior from him, let him know that you'll leave if it happens again, get his agreement to stop acting this way, and follow through with what you said you'd do if he ever does it again.

SEVENTY-SIX

My coworkers ignore me. What should I do?

How should I deal with coworkers that ignore me? I tend to isolate myself during breaks and such, so that leads to more ignoring. And I think I should address the situation because I'm new at the job and I don't feel welcome. Any tips would be nice.

You sound like an introvert, and introverts can be perceived as arrogant and uninterested. I'm sure you don't intend to give that impression, so here are ten tips you may want to try:

1. **Be approachable.** Smile, make eye contact, and show interest in getting to know your coworkers.

2. **Initiate conversations.** Don't wait for others to approach you. Strike up conversations and ask about their jobs and interests. If you want people to be interested in you, you must show interest in them.

3. **Learn names.** Remembering names helps create a personal connection and shows you value your coworkers. Dale Carnegie said that "**a person's name is the sweetest sound they can hear**" in his famous book *How to Win Friends and Influence People*.

4. **Be open.** Share some personal information, hobbies, or interests to help others relate to you.

5. **Listen actively.** Pay attention when others talk and respond thoughtfully to show you value their input.

6. **Participate in social activities.** Attend team lunches, outings, and other events to build relationships outside of work activities.

7. **Ask for help.** Don't hesitate to ask questions or seek guidance. It demonstrates your eagerness to learn and engage.

8. **Offer help.** When appropriate, offer your help to your colleagues. It's a great way to bond and showcase your skills.

9. **Show appreciation.** Express gratitude for help received and acknowledge contributions made by others.

10. **Stay positive.** Maintain a positive attitude, even in challenging situations. Your optimism will be contagious.

Most importantly, remember that building relationships takes time, so be patient and persistent in your efforts to feel welcome. I wish you well.

SEVENTY-SEVEN

Someone, please tell me what to do.

I and my husband are currently going through one of the worst periods of our lives.

We just had to move in with my grandparents. I had to give my ex the kids this year for school because I can't support them. My account is almost $340 in the hole and, at this exact moment, I'm stranded about 20 miles away from my kids.

I went to work this morning, and because I was exactly 14 minutes late (security was super slow), they sent me home. I gave someone a ride yesterday and I was supposed to get gas money, but I never saw them.

So now I'm just stuck here. I feel like I've just lost control of every facet of my life. I can't breathe. I've been diagnosed with like seven different anxiety and mood disorders, and when I tell my psychiatrist this, she just says, "Well, I'll see you next month. Good luck!" This was her exact response to "I'm having between 5-7 panic attacks a day. The heart palpitations are awful and constant."

I just feel like I can't fix anything. I feel like I can't move or breathe. And yesterday I started just randomly crying. I honestly didn't think I had anymore tears to cry. Someone tell me this gets easier. I'm gonna be 30 in three days. Every day just feels harder and harder. I'm blessed to have my partner, though. He's been my rock—the only thing keeping my head above water.

I know a lot of people have been in this spot, and they climb out of it. But how do you do that when you can't even get to work? Sorry this is all over the place. I know I'm a mess. Thanks.

I'm going to ask you a series of questions with the hope that the answers you provide will guide you to what you need. Ultimately, though, you seem to be experiencing a sense of self-powerlessness, and I hope to help you take your power back.

Does your husband contribute to the household? You never mention that he does. If he doesn't, is it because he can't work due to a disability? If he's disabled, has he applied for benefits? If he's disabled and hasn't applied for benefits, he should do that as soon as possible, so that your financial situation can improve. If he does contribute to the household, is he willing to look for a higher paying job, and if not, why? If he doesn't have a disability and just doesn't work to help support the family, he hasn't been the support you claim him to be. If all he has is a series of excuses, they'll be no help in changing your situation.

Have you (and your husband) taken full responsibility for the financial situation you're in, or do you both blame someone (or something) else? Going over the things you've mentioned, you said your account balance is -$340. How did it get there? Did you overspend, not paying attention to what was actually in the account? Do you keep up with the balance in your account, or do you just spend money that you hope is there? If the latter, you'll continue to have money problems, and that's something you must take responsibility for. If you can't afford a lifestyle, wishing and hoping the money will be there to pay for it won't make it so.

You said you were 14 minutes late for work and blamed it on the slowness of security. One of the things you must account for when deciding how much time it takes to get to work is that you may need more time to get through security. If you end up at work a little early, it makes you look good. Whether you're early or on time, though, it's still your responsibility to leave earlier than you have been.

Even if the person you gave a ride hasn't paid you gas money, your finances shouldn't be so shaky that $20 (or so) makes or breaks you. Obviously, they're not the reason you're in your current financial situation.

The psychiatrist, assuming they are competent, sees something that doesn't allow them to acknowledge your diagnosis. Who diagnosed you? Because it doesn't sound like this psychiatrist did. In fact, it doesn't sound like the psychiatrist has any medical documentation showing you have these diagnoses. Their response to your heart palpitations seem to show that they don't believe what you're experiencing is a medical condition—if they believed it was, they'd advise you to seek medical treatment. Rather, it seemed they didn't really know how to respond.

Since you said you feel like you've lost control of every facet of your life, it seems you don't feel in charge of it—in fact, it seems that you feel like life is something that simply happens to you and over which you have no control. Viktor Frankl, in his book *Man's Search for Meaning*, said something that I use as a check to make sure that I'm not simply letting life happen to me, but that I remain in charge of my life. He said, **"Ultimately, man should not ask what the meaning of his**

life is, but rather must recognize that it is he who is asked. In a word, each man is questioned by life; and he can only answer to life by answering for his own life; to life he can only respond by being responsible."

How do you get through this? How does it get easier? Let me ask you this: as the saying goes, how do you eat an elephant? One bite at a time. Pick one thing of the many you want to change, decide to change it, including writing down the steps you'll take, then do those steps. For instance, if you want to tackle getting to work on time, and you were 14 minutes late, you may decide that you'll leave the house 20 (or even 30!) minutes earlier than you have been, then work backwards from there deciding when you'll get up, how long it'll take to get ready, etc. That's you taking charge of your life!

Once you get one thing tackled, work on the next, then the next. For instance, where your finances are concerned, you may want to create a budget based off your actual income and stick to it. Taking steps like these will make you feel more and more self-empowered, and the more success you have, the more empowered you'll feel, and it'll become easier to feel in control of your life. This is how you'll respond to life by being responsible.

SEVENTY-EIGHT

I'm middle aged and totally lost in life.

I'm going to be 40 years old next year, and my life completely sucks. I have no family, no friends, no hobbies, never been in a relationship, still a virgin, have Avoidant Personality Disorder, work a dead-end job, and I'm currently living in a cheap motel, am overweight and overwhelmed, and don't know how to fix it.

Most people whose life is this much of a mess make terrible decisions. They either get hooked on drugs or go to prison—not me. Every time I try something it goes sideways. I've moved over 30 times and attended 26 different schools growing up, so when I would try to make friends or join a club, I would be zipped off to another school. My sister was six years older and a child of divorce, and as soon as she got into middle school, she was off doing what rebellious children of divorce do and had no interest in spending time with her younger sibling, and as soon as she turned eighteen, she left and never looked back.

Mom had no time or patience for me and just tolerated me until I was 18, then kicked me out. By the time I pulled myself out of homelessness, I was in my mid-20s—renting a section of a basement, working in a fast food job, overworked, and depressed.

After thirteen years of scraping by, I found a job that pays more. I finally had enough money to get my own apartment. Then the pandemic hit, and I was lucky to have an essential job and making money. I can't have nice things and my apartment burned down.

Now, I'm on the verge of ending it all. I left out a lot of details, but every time I try something new, I fail, and something goes wrong that knocks me right back to the start.

I really don't think I can make it to 41. I'm on the verge of ending it.

This may seem unpleasant to do, but I'll ask you to examine your words. You said that your life completely sucks. Does it *completely suck*? Has there been no single good thing to ever happen to you? Your self-talk is negative, and that'll never, ever produce a positive outcome.

As you look over your life, recall at least one thing that went your way. One thing. Once you have that thing in mind, describe it to yourself. Imagine yourself in that situation again. How do you feel now? Have your feelings changed, even slightly? Whether they have or haven't, now imagine one more good thing that has happened to you in the 39 years you've lived. How does reliving that time in your mind make you feel? Any better?

Even in the most unpleasant of circumstances, we can recall good moments that have happened in our lives. No one has ever existed for 39 years without having at least one good thing happen to them. What's my point? How you interpret the world around you is exactly how it'll be, and if you want to change your experience of the world, you must change your interpretation.

There's a story told of a man who fell asleep on a couch. While asleep, his child thought it would be funny to smear limburger cheese in his moustache. When he woke up, he smelled an awful scent. He sat up, sniffed around the area, and exclaimed, "This room *stinks!*" He walked to the next room, sniffed, and shouted, "This room stinks, too!" He walked through the whole house, sniffing from room to room, and declared, "This house stinks!" He then walked outside, sniffed thoughtfully, and decided, "The whole world stinks!"

This is how thoughts work. Thoughts can be the limburger cheese of our perception, or they can produce gratitude by revealing good things. Not only have good things happened to you, but by your own admission you've overcome the temptation to make terrible decisions like being hooked on drugs or going to prison.

If you choose to begin to focus on the good things that have happened to you, they'll produce more good things, just as focusing on the bad things that have happened to you produced more bad things. No friends? Who'd want to be around someone who's always negative? I'm sure you don't even want to be around yourself sometimes, since you speak of ending it all, so why would someone else want to be around you as you are now?

I understand that, at 39 years of age, you look back over your life and ask yourself what you have done with it, and if you aren't happy with where you are in life, you fall into despair. But the answer isn't more negativity. That hasn't produced anything good for you, and it never will. You can't grow a bitter tree and expect sweet fruit, no matter how many years you've spent tending it.

What do you do now? You challenge your thoughts. No one's life *completely* sucks, not even yours. For what are you grateful? There's nothing to be done about the past, or what your parents have done, or your apartment having burnt down, but what law says you can't have nice things? That's something you made up that you have the power to change! Just like having failed doesn't make you a failure if you don't give up.

It doesn't matter how many times you fail at doing things—what matters is that you succeed the last time you try, and you won't have a chance to succeed if you give up because you've been failing.

I speak as someone whose life has been to hell and back more times than I care to count—and this is not just a pep speech, I promise, but I mean it from the bottom of my heart—**you've got the rest of your life to make the best of your life!**

SEVENTY-NINE

A guy asked me what didn't click for me after a date. Should I be honest?

I went out for a date last night. We met on a dating app. His pictures made him look a bit different, and he was extremely kind over text. When we met, I was surprised to see he was a much bigger person that his photos led me to believe, and I noticed he smelled pretty bad...like sweat.

He was very nice. We went out, then went bowling and continued to talk. After the date, he texted me saying he had a wonderful time and wanted to see me again, and I was honest with him. I told him I wasn't really feeling it but would like to remain friends.

I feel like the girl in all those ridiculous posts people make. He drove an hour to meet me, paid our bill at the bowling alley before I had a chance to object. And I barely gave him anything other than a rejection. I feel awful! He's a super kind person and I feel like I really screwed him over, but obviously I'm not going to force myself to do stuff with him that makes me uncomfortable. That's unfair to both of us.

He asked me what it was about him that didn't click for me, as he's always trying to improve himself. I don't think telling him, "You're bigger than I expected and smell bad, so I wasn't attracted to you" is a fair thing to say, but I honestly can't think of anything else.

He's a perfect gentleman, opened doors for me, asked permission to place his arm around me, a great listener, and funny and charming. I think he's got the personality down pat but, again, I can't force myself to feel attraction.

I also want to be concrete in that I'm not interested, and I don't want to waste his time. Ugh! What do I say?

As a guy, I can tell you that if a man asks you for things that don't make him work for you, he wants to know, and you should tell him. Guys who ask really do appreciate knowing. Besides, it would be a great way to give him something he could really use.

It's great that he asked instead of just becoming an incel, pitying himself, hating women, and loathing men who are more successful at dating.

There are people who would continue to spend time with someone they're not interested in simply to keep from hurting their feelings, no matter how uncomfortable it makes *them* feel. I'm glad to see that you're not that kind of person. Staying with someone you're not interested in does that person no favors, because you'll eventually reach the point where you can't take it anymore, and you'll break it off—except this will come when that person has much deeper feelings for you than if you'd just been honest in the first place.

So yes, you should be honest, and **there are ways to do it without being cruel.** One way is by making it a sandwich.

What do I mean?

Just as a sandwich has bread on both ends and meat (or something other than bread) in the middle, the sandwich method consists of beginning and ending the feedback with positive things, while the middle contains information where he can improve. In other words, tell him the good things you noticed about him, tell him what he can improve, and then tell him how improving those things would make him great to be with.

For instance, you talked about how nice he is, how he's a perfect gentleman, how he opened your door for you, asked permission to place his arm around you, is a great listener, as well as how funny and charming he is. That's a great way to start the feedback. Then you can let him know that you found his odor off-putting, as well as your surprise when you found out he was bigger than his photos. You could end with the thought that, if he combined better hygiene and recent photos with all the other outstanding traits he has, he would be a great catch for someone.

EIGHTY

Should I change my job if I'm not happy, but it makes more money than what I want to switch to?

I'm 28, and I've been working in an office environment IT job for the past two years. I come from a family of blue-collar working men that are in the trades, so my whole life I grew up helping my dad, grandfather, and stepdad on weekends and summers, sometimes doing electrical work and flooring.

I turned 18 and joined the Navy as an electrician and got out at 23 and found a job as a civilian working as an assembler while going to school for IT. At 26, I got a job in IT and have been there for two years. I really only pursued this career for money, if I'm being honest, and I'm coming to realize that I'm not interested in it at all and feel extremely unsatisfied and unfulfilled at work.

Sitting behind the desk and computer all day makes me miserable, and I look around at some of my coworkers and they look like zombies and don't seem happy with their lives. And the day absolutely seems longer than it is, with 8-hour days feeling like 12-hour days.

I know being an electrician and working in the trades is hard work and hard on the body and I'd also have to take a slight pay cut in the beginning, but I think I'm most fulfilled and happy when I'm moving around and working with my hands.

Do you have any advice?

Yes. Though it may not seem so right now at 28, life's too short to waste happiness and fulfillment for money. The only purpose more money serves is to have more things, and is it better to have more things and be miserable, or have less things and be happy? After all, **how does one achieve happiness—by having more, or by wanting less?**

It sounds like you'll feel much more fulfilled if you went back to being an electrician. I'm sure the nostalgia of having done it with your dad, stepdad, and grandfather, along with how productive you'll feel working with your hands, and how quickly you'll be able to produce evidence of a job well done, will make you feel happier and more rewarded. You'll feel more productive than you do now by tapping on a keyboard all day long.

Do what you love, and you'll be rich in all the ways that matter.

EIGHTY-ONE

I think a breakup put me in a midlife crisis.

I'm recently single again after almost four years with someone I thought I would end up with for the rest of my life. The breakup was my choice, but now that I've made my decision, it makes me think about other life choices. A lot.

We had a house together which I'm moving out of. I'm staying at a friend's house in another city for a few weeks until I can find my own place. As I'm here (the same city where my siblings, parents, and friends live), I realize I'd prefer to move back here. That would mean I have to commute to work for 2-3 hours per day in total, but I can't see myself starting over in the town where I work.

Immediately I start thinking about whether I should change jobs as well if I'm moving anyway. The job I have now is okay but not great, and I'll probably end up with a lower salary if I quit. It's just that I honestly don't know what work I want to do. How do you find that out? Trying to work my way to something I'd enjoy doing most days, I end up dreaming *of a different kind of life completely, with more freedom and flexibility, and with someone by my side.*

This somehow brings me right into the 'what relationship am I ever going to end up in, if any' thoughts. Will I just have to make peace with staying single? I feel like I'm no longer believing the vision of me finding a partner to share my life with, and I'm also unsure of the whole child thing. Which feels stressful, because I'm getting old in fertility terms, and I want to make a choice and not have it made for me. Then again, I don't want to jump into a new relationship—I need time.

Right about there I start questioning my decision to break up, but I had reasons and then this circle of thoughts is complete. I don't know what I want, what to do, or where to begin to find out. Do you have some advice?

Feeling overwhelmed after making the right decision doesn't mean that it wasn't the right decision. Even feeling overwhelmed with the enormity of what a breakup means when it involves so many aspects (moving out of the comfort of your home, moving to another city, considering changing jobs, wondering if you'll ever have another relationship, the Poeish telltale ticking of your biological clock) is daunting. Let's take each of your concerns one at a time.

The city you've moved to has family and friends that provide you with emotional support. That's important, and something so precious that it's not to be taken for granted. From what you write, it seems you prefer to move there permanently.

Since that's what you'd like to do, your next question is whether you should change jobs. You have a twofold concern: that you may take a cut in pay, and that you don't know what you want to do for employment. Let's tackle those by talking about the last concern first.

How do you find out what you want to do in life? A good question to ask yourself is this: what would you do that'd make you happy, even if you didn't get paid to do it? What is your dream? The answer to that question describes your passion. If you can find a job that aligns itself with your passion, you'll be one of the most fortunate of persons. If you can find a job that trains you to carry out your passion, that's equally fortunate. If you can't, you may be able to find a job that allows you the freedom and flexibility you crave. Perhaps a remote job can allow you that freedom and flexibility so that, even if it doesn't align with your passion, it'll at least give you the freedom and flexibility to work your passion on the side.

Now to your other concern: ending up with a lower salary. As you said, you *may* end up with a lower salary—there's no guarantee that you will. I don't think that's as much of a concern for you as knowing *what* you want to do, but even if you take a salary cut, you'll be happier—you'll feel free, and those are things money can't buy.

As to the question of what relationship you're going to end up in, if any—my question to you is this: how do you want to be if you begin another relationship—happy or frustrated with yourself? Because **if you're not happy with yourself, you won't be happy in a relationship** (you may be temporarily distracted by the newness of being in a relationship, but that's not the same as happiness), so your happiness, contentment, peace, and self-love come first. As you do those things that communicate that you love yourself, you become the whole, emotionally healthy person that's an asset to a relationship with another person *and* in an incredible relationship with yourself. With this level of self-relationship, you'll be content, whether it's alone, with a partner, or with a child.

There's no one that can guarantee whether you'll be alone or with someone (other than you), but you'll be sure to avoid someone who isn't good for you if you treat yourself with such love that you won't settle for being treated any less from someone else. And any child that's a recipient of such love (if that's in your future) will be fortunate, indeed.

EIGHTY-TWO

I lost $800, and it's hard not to hate myself for it.

I *lost $800 by not filling out a stupid 3-minute claim for a class action*
lawsuit. The claim submission expired four days ago, and it was
very easy money.

My hours at work have been cut repeatedly, and life has felt like it's
running in fast forward.

I started to submit a claim a week ago, but I was doing something else
while I was on my phone, put my phone down, and forgot about it till
days later when it expired.

So this was a huge blow. I don't know what to do. $800 can make a
huge *difference for my current situation, and to lose that because of my*
own negligence makes me feel helpless. On top of all my depression I've
managed the last week, this hit me ten times harder, making me feel a
boiling hatred for myself and my stupidity.

If we had the power to change the past, I'm sure everyone would change *something* about it—a decision made, a direction taken, a word said. Those of us who were extremely abused or suffered some devastating moments in our pasts would love to be able to go back and change them somehow. We can drive ourselves crazy wishing that something had been different. We can become angry, bitter, or depressed about something we wish, with all our power, we could change, and all we'll have to show for it is trading what *can* change (our presents and futures) for what *can't* change (our pasts).

Is there *any* way possible to get the $800 from the past? There's no way to get it, so the only thing left to do is to accept that it happened. To accept it is to realize that no amount of self-hate, no amount of emotional self-torture, and no amount of regret will get you that $800, so all that's left is to accept that it happened and can't be changed. If it could, I'd be calling myself stupid all day! Take a deep breath and, as you exhale, let go of what's impossible to retrieve—the past.

To take this another step, **love yourself by forgiving yourself.** This boiling hatred is an attempt to punish yourself for something that is no longer in your control. How long will you punish yourself? At some point, you must pardon yourself for your mistake and set yourself free from it. Hating yourself and calling yourself stupid won't bring you $800, and it'll only make you miserable, so what's the point?

Yes, the $800 would've made a huge difference in your current situation, but is there any other time that you felt that you were in a circumstance that you couldn't see any way out of? Have you ever told yourself there's no way you can make it through something? How many of those have you made it through in the past? 100%!! So that's proof that you can do it again!

We can become so used to generating self-talk that reminds us of all the things we've done *wrong* that we don't realize we can use that same power to remind ourselves of all the things we've done *right*. They're both in your power, and one cripples you while the other empowers you. Which will you choose?

Is it easy? No. Is it easier said than done? Yes. But that's no excuse to keep from doing the work. It's hard, but the more you practice, the easier it gets, just like most other things in life. Don't let the fact that it's hard keep you from doing what will bring you contentment, happiness, self-love, and peace.

EIGHTY-THREE

How do I learn to no longer depend on being codependent?

I got divorced last year and I've been trying to improve myself, but it seems like I'm getting nowhere. Before my marriage, I was on the brink of ending my life, and she saved me. I believe we were both in similar situations, so we ended up just being codependent. After eight years, we decided to split, and now I'm back to being depressed.

I've been dating this other girl for the past three months who got divorced last year, as well. She thinks that we both need to stop what we're doing and not be serious, but I have already fallen for her.

How do I: 1) stop having an anxious attachment style; 2) learn to love myself; and 3) be okay with being alone?

As you know, an anxious attachment style comes from feeling abandoned as a child by your parents or caregivers, whether physically or emotionally. It arises from believing that, since your caregivers didn't think you were worth giving attention to, no one else will. As a result, while you desire intimacy, you find it difficult to trust others, you fear getting emotionally close to someone else, you find it difficult to maintain your boundaries, you need constant reassurance, you find yourself being obsessive or clingy, and/or you become anxious when you're not physically near your partner. This anxiety can easily lead into people-pleasing behaviors, as the fear of rejection overpowers the ability to love yourself or recognize your own needs.

'If I could just find someone to give me the affection I crave, I'd be happy' is your mantra, while doubting the permanence of that affection. Tying your happiness to things outside your control, however, is a recipe for disaster. **There's no way to *control* things that are outside your control, no matter how anxious, desperate, or depressed you become.**

The key to overcoming such a style is by realizing that 1) nothing and no one can fill a hole created by the past; 2) it's what you've been *telling yourself* about the relationships you've entered into that has made you anxious and prematurely attached; 3) you must forgive those who didn't give you the affection you needed, realizing that there has to be a reason why, and that reason has nothing to do with you being undeserving of it or it in any way being your fault; and 4) you must learn to love yourself and enjoy your own company, because if you don't love being with yourself, how can you expect anyone else to love being with you?

Before discussing how to love yourself, though, let's break these four things down a little more.

The past is gone. You're left with a void, a need that wasn't fulfilled. There's nothing to be done about it, and no one can fill a past void. When you let go of the idea that you'll fill the hole that was left by the past, you'll begin to gain power over an anxious attachment in the present.

On the other hand, if what you tell yourself sounds something like, "She must love me, and if she doesn't, I can't stand it," or "If she doesn't love me, it's because I'm unlovable, and I'll always be alone and miserable," you'll have an anxious attachment that will cause one of the biggest turnoffs for women—desperation. Thoughts like these playing over and over in your head will make you absolutely unhappy. Challenge these kinds of thoughts. Why must she love you? Is it a rule or a law? How many situations have you been in where you've said to yourself, "I can't stand this?" What would happen if that was true—if you really couldn't stand something? You'd die, and since you're not dead, you've stood everything you said you couldn't up until now, so the evidence shows that you *can* stand it. And is it true that you'll always be alone and miserable? How do you know? Can you predict the future? What if you changed those thoughts to "It would be nice if she loved me, but I'll survive if she doesn't" or "I deserve love just like any other person, and I can't predict if I'll be alone, but I can work on not thinking things that make me miserable"? Please understand that this isn't an overnight transition by any means. Years of harmful thinking must be replaced, and that takes time and effort. I suggest you work on this every day by placing notes around your house, car, etc., with the thoughts written on them that you want to replace the bad ones with and read them to yourself every time you see them.

Forgive those who didn't give you the affection you needed. It's easy to blame them for the hole you feel, but realize that they have their own holes, too. Whether it was their inability to give what they didn't have, the hurt they felt as they faced their own pasts, or their inattention to you as they dealt with their own pain, it's not your fault that you didn't get the love you needed. You were never unworthy of that love. Don't hate them for what they didn't give you; realize they didn't have it to give. However, remember that you *are* worthy of love, but that love must first come from within.

How do you learn to love yourself? This is such a great question! The reason I think it's such a good question is that some people confuse self-love with self-preservation. What do I mean? For instance, if you and a stranger were kidnapped and the kidnapper pointed a gun at you and told you to choose whether you'd die or the stranger, who wouldn't choose the stranger? But that's self-preservation, not self-love.

Self-love, on the other hand, is giving yourself the mercy, grace, compassion, and forgiveness you'd give to those you love the most. It's treating yourself the way you'd treat your best friend. For instance, if your best friend called you at two in the morning because they were dealing with a crisis that they couldn't figure out, would you scold them, or would you help them? Would you be angry at them, or would you treat them with compassion, staying up with them and reassuring them? Self-love would treat you the way you'd treat them, having the same compassion for yourself and mercy on yourself you'd have for them.

So how do you learn to love yourself? You begin by realizing *that you want to love yourself.* The fact that you even *want* to love yourself, and what you want isn't impossible to achieve, is evidence that it's something a part of you realizes you *should* have. Once you accept that it's something you should have, next comes the work. This is the work: telling yourself continuously, "I'm worthy of love, and it must begin with me. If I don't love myself, how can I expect anyone else to love me? If I don't find myself lovable, how can I expect anyone else to find me lovable? Since I want love, there's a part of me telling myself that I'm lovable, and I'll listen to that part." Write down the reasons you deserve to love yourself and remind yourself continuously of those reasons. Realize that the people who made you feel unlovable simply didn't have the love to give, because they didn't love themselves.

Love needs to be an overflowing cup, and it's from the overflow of self-love that we give to others. If our cup's empty or only partially full, there's nothing to give to others, and if they don't feel loved, they'll go where love overflows in someone else so they can be loved. Make your cup overflow, and you'll not only love yourself—you'll have love to spare.

EIGHTY-FOUR

Is how my husband treats me acceptable?

My husband and I have been married for eight years. We have a one-year-old and bought our first home together about a year ago. He gets VA disability and Social Security for mental issues, and I work full time.

Since we've gotten married, I've done virtually all the household chores (cook, clean, care for the pets and now baby, etc.). He doesn't do anything around the house, and he expects me to do it all because he makes more than I do working. We have a joint bank account where all our money goes, but he still lashes out at me about financial issues and says, "You don't make enough or contribute enough to ask me to do any of the household chores". We've had a pretty rough past in our marriage, but I'm in therapy and I'm trying to work through it all for our family.

I don't know what to do because I'm feeling so drained physically, mentally, and emotionally. Any advice?

I'm going to make some assumptions here, since I've never met you and haven't lived in your situation with you. It's based on how I imagine your day-to-day life is with him.

Your husband disrespects himself because he thinks he's "less than a man" since he's not able to work to provide for his family, and he's projecting that disrespect for himself onto you by disrespecting you. He's so miserable and self-pitying that he has tunnel vision, not being able to see beyond himself and his situation.

His basing your ability to require anything of him on how much money you contribute, compared to him, is just an excuse. It's a way to get you to stop asking him to do things around the house. What he doesn't realize, though, is that his contributing to the needs of the house, as well as to your happiness, should be out of the love that he feels for you and his desire for your happiness. He's too far into his own pity party to recognize what should be his commitment to the household.

As he has mental issues, it would be appropriate for him to be in therapy, which is free through the VA, but it sounds like he's not taking advantage of that free medical care. If he were in therapy, a therapist would help him differentiate the pain he feels because of his own emotional wounds from the pain he thinks he derives from you asking him to help around the house, and I recommend you talk to him about taking advantage of that free VA therapy.

You stated your reason for being in therapy is "I'm trying to work through it all for our family". The greatest benefit therapy can have for the family is when the family is in therapy together. Whatever benefits you get from therapy (and it's great that you're going through therapy) are primarily for you. They won't benefit him. He must seek help to benefit from therapy. If he benefits from you going to therapy, at best it'll be minimal.

What he sees as "doing any of the household chores" could be reinterpreted as ways to show how much he loves you. His care, concern, and help would speak volumes. You do these things for him and your family to show your love for them, and he doesn't, leaving you feeling unloved, which contributes to your feeling drained emotionally, mentally, and physically.

What can you do? **You can explain to him that his help with chores is about love, not money, or who makes the most.** If he insists on making money the indicator of whether he should help, you can let him know that the work you do at home is worth $184,820 per year, according to the latest figures, and ask him if your full-time salary combined with your housework "salary" is greater than what he brings home in benefits. I'm willing to bet it isn't.

EIGHTY-FIVE

I want to know my father. Am I being stupid?

*M*y father left when I was two years old, and ever since my mother passed away in 2016, I don't have any family. I had a sister, but she's been cut out of my life due to how toxic she is. She has a father in her life who was also terrible, but she still has him and talks about him all the time.

*The problem with my father is that the reason he left was because he got arrested and sent to prison. What I'm about to say is a **very** sensitive subject, but the reason he went away is because he molested someone.*

I know where he lives, but I'm not sure what to do. Am I jealous of my sister for having her dad around, or am I just being stupid?

It's completely natural to want to have a relationship with your father, no matter what he's done in the past. No matter how hurt, overwhelmed, amazed, or disappointed we are at our parents' behavior, there's usually a part of us that yearns for their love despite those other feelings. Sometimes we may even try to deny or suppress those feelings, but then we have trouble understanding why we're depressed, self-loathing, angry, bitter, or lashing out uncharacteristically at others.

Whether it's a desire to have a relationship with him to see how similar or different you both are, or to see if he missed you when he went to prison and wants a relationship with you but is too ashamed to ask for one, **there's nothing wrong with your desire to get to know him.** It really doesn't even have as much to do with any jealousy for your sister's relationship with *her* father as it does your desire for a relationship with *yours*.

If you decide that you want to begin a relationship with your father, make sure that you want to do it for the right reason. For instance, if you want to see him for the sole purpose of unleashing your pent-up anger at him for being absent and have no intention of listening to him, it's the wrong reason, but if your heart longs for a relationship with him, it's the right one.

If you're doing it for the right reason, pursue the relationship, but understand that he may not feel the same way you do. I hope he will but be prepared in case he doesn't.

What do I mean?

When we long for something really badly, we can't help but imagine what it'll be like. Usually, we think of something like a reunion as being joyous, our hearts bursting with love as we embrace the one we missed for so long. However, things don't always go that way, and when they don't, and we've imagined the moment as being wonderful for so long, we're devastated. If we prepare ourselves for both eventualities by imagining both scenarios, though, we allow ourselves to go into something like a reunion (at least somewhat) ready to deal with it, no matter which way it goes.

I wish you the best!

EIGHTY-SIX

Why do I want to leave it all and move away so badly?

I own my own home, have a very well-paying job, and a long-term relationship with a person who would be any girl's dream husband (by that I mean he has a great job, he's smart, he holds his own weight, he's a good roommate, has a good family, etc.).

And what I don't get is why I feel this drastic, unshakable urge to leave it all. It has grown from a small, fleeting thought to an all-consuming issue. I even started taking anti-anxiety medication, wondering if that could be my issue.

The main thing is probably location. I live in a mid-sized Midwest city. Both my significant other and I grew up here, and our families are here. He's content staying put here, probably for the rest of his life. But I feel a great need to leave, go to a bigger city, experience downtown city living, etc., and most of our friends have gone off, moved to new cities, and started their own adventures. And I feel like I skipped all my 20s *fun and hopped right into a safe, peaceful, and (unfortunately) boring life.*

I took a job a few months ago and, while I love it and the pay, it's not the type of position that's easy to uproot from (local clients, sales, etc.). I also have a mortgage on a home, which makes me feel stuck as well. And for the most part I can't shake the feeling that this just isn't what I was meant to be doing with my life—the life I should be so content and grateful for. I have all the things I need and more, great relationships, and everything. So why on earth do I have this feeling to obliterate it all, jump ship, and move away?

You feel the need to create expansive memories, adventures, and experience more of what life has to offer. You want to feel the excitement of taking a chance on a new chapter instead of remaining in your current, predictable one.

The world is big, and the varieties of experiences available to you are immeasurably greater than all that you could experience in a mid-sized Midwest city. It sounds like you have wanderlust, which is amazing, and you're not alone. Much has been said about picking up and experiencing life somewhere else, from "A change of latitude would help my attitude" (unknown); "To travel is to live" (Hans Christian Anderson); "Life begins at the end of your comfort zone" (Neale Donald Walsch); "We travel not to escape life, but for life not to escape us" (anonymous); "It's a big world out there—it would be a shame not to experience it" (J. D. Andrews); "The world is a book, and those who do not travel read only one page" (St. Augustine); to "Adventure may hurt you, but monotony will kill you" (Ghaniya Dewi Arassy).

Which leads me to my proposed solution—have you planned any vacations with your husband? If not, will you? It could begin by visiting big cities, creating memories and having adventures there, then moving on to international travel.

Planning and taking vacations will allow you to remain in your mid-sized Midwest city while experiencing the sensation of jumping ship and moving away for a few days or a week or two every now and then. As you save for your next destination, you'll dream of undiscovered shores, exciting lands, and invaluable reminiscences. You'll savor new memories while satisfying your wanderlust, and you'll return home refreshed, revitalized, and contented. I've had incredible opportunities to travel to many foreign countries and across the United States, and I've been made a richer man for doing so. It has impacted me exponentially while allowing me to be content living in a small Southern U.S. town. I wouldn't be who I am today without the multitude of my experiences!

As someone said, **"Always remember—presence is far more important than presents, and magic comes from memories, not stuff."** I believe that not only applies to being present in the lives of our loved ones, but also to breaking free from the tedium of daily life to create memories. May your memories surpass both your marvel and your money!

EIGHTY-SEVEN

My wife always feels the need to fill empty air with conversation, even at the expense of making everyone else uncomfortable.

*E*very time we're with family or close friends, my wife compulsively either initiates a thought experiment (e.g., would you rather this or that?), or shares random intimate information about me or her. Emphasis on poor timing and an inability to read the room. This always happens once conversation has died down and all the "heavy hitter" topics have been worn out.

For example, during a recent family get together, we had finished dinner and were sitting on the couch making small talk and a silence appeared, so she happily informed everyone that I had started taking out my contacts nightly. It was met with mostly silence as I scrambled to explain what she just said and change the topic.

Any tips?

Have you asked her why she does this? If you have, perhaps she's said something like she doesn't want family or guests to become uncomfortable or bored. Since you haven't mentioned that she mainly does this when she's the host of an event, I'll assume that she does it whether she's hosting or just attending something.

She may be doing it to feel liked or validated. By doing what she believes will make sure people are happy, she may feel as if she's useful or valued.

As you describe the conversation about the contacts, a reasonable person would've realized that revealing that information the way she did makes others uncomfortable by their response. As it sounds like she often does this despite how others respond, it could be that she panics when there's silence. Why would she do that? **She may see silence as scary because thoughts and emotions can flood in when they're not distracted by noise.**

I would recommend that, since this seems to be something she feels she needs to do, sit down with her and discuss topics to bring up when there's a lull in conversation, or even suggest games like charades or "Guess Who I Am/20 Questions" to the group. The main thing is that you both discuss this ahead of time, so you can agree on topics she brings up when there's silence.

Also, you may consider bearing some of the burden for keeping conversation flowing in the group instead of having to step in when she does something potentially embarrassing and having to carry the conversation anyway. If you choose to do this, let her know that this is what you'll be doing (but not why). She'll appreciate some of the load being taken off of her, I'm sure.

EIGHTY-EIGHT

I can't form strong relationships, and the people who should care about me don't. My life is so small—how do I make it feel better?

I'm married with two kids. First, my husband is wonderful and tries, but I can't make him my whole social world. I've got a large family, but for the past few months I've been drifting from them, and it feels like they don't care about me anymore. I don't like the same things most of them do, but I try really hard to find connections. They don't seem to do the same with me or include me if they don't have to. Lately, I can be at a family gathering and not speak for an hour beyond taking care of my children, and no one notices.

My friend group is really, really small, because I haven't been able to hold on to any adult relationships beyond three people with whom I went to high school. They have kids and busy lives of their own, so it's not like they actually ignore me, but they don't initiate any of the contact, and while I try to make time for them, they usually don't do the same. I've tried making friends over the years, but they don't last beyond whatever initiated contact (e.g., job, book club that ended, league team, etc.).

I work from home part time and haven't been able to find a new job since the pandemic started. I got a couple of interviews that went well, and one interviewer even told me it wasn't a matter of if but when they could hire me, but they all ghosted me.

I feel like my life has gotten so small that I'm just nothing anymore except a mom with nothing for myself. I don't know why it seems like I'm inoffensive but inconsequential. Please help me figure out how to make my life more than this.

It sounds like you crave interaction with others and have so much to give. Please allow me a moment to be as gentle as I can with what I'm about to say, but I want you to know that what I'm about to tell you is something that has made all the difference in my own life.

I spent decades drowning in my own misery. I was unhappy, unfulfilled, miserable, upset, self-pitying, and alone. Even being married with children, I was alone. I tried my best being different things for different people in an attempt to win them over, and I'm sure my desperation repelled them all—a desperation evidenced by a desire to be impressive while seeking love and acceptance.

In my book *Things I Wish My Father Had Told Me* I describe the Law of Multiplication when it comes to romantic relationships. That is, people often go into relationships looking for their other half, believing that their half plus the other person's half will make a whole, or ½ + ½ will equal 1. However, these relationships don't follow the Law of Addition, but the Law of Multiplication. In other words, instead of the two halves making a whole, each half desperately seeks to get what they don't have from the other half. With both halves reaching and grasping, no one is satisfied, and the state of that person ends up being less than before they entered the relationship— ½ times ½, which is ¼. This law works as well, or as poorly, for non-romantic relationships.

Following that same law, when a whole person enters a relationship with another whole person, their wholeness continues—in other words, 1 times 1 equals 1. But it begins with finding your wholeness before you look outside yourself. How do you begin? That's something I didn't discuss in the book, but I will talk about here, but before I do, I want to answer this question—why look for your own wholeness first?

You can't give from an empty cup, and you shouldn't give of yourself from a partially filled cup. Trying to give of yourself from a partially filled cup is the same as trying to desperately get filled by someone else who has a partially filled cup. Someone ends up with less than they began, which makes their situation worse.

However, I'm not even proposing giving of yourself from a filled cup—I propose that you wait until your cup is *overflowing* before you give from it! If you give from a filled cup, it's not longer filled, but if you give from your overflow, you remain filled—you remain whole. Here are some strategies to achieve wholeness.

It begins with believing, with no doubt mixed in, that you *deserve* wholeness. This can be especially tough for anyone who's used to being abused, misused, or treated less than they deserve—whether this is true in their current relationships, or they experienced this as children. For me, my father put up with so much from his relationships without demanding that he be treated the way he deserved in the name of keeping peace—which I learned from him. For so long, I accepted less than I deserved—the vast majority of my life. I finally realized that to truly love myself and create an overflow in my heart, I had to realize I was worthy of so much more than I received, and I had to refuse to settle for less! By doing this, I gave myself what I wasn't receiving, and I created wholeness in myself despite what others refused to give. I felt lighter, freer—and, in turn, that was the impression I gave wherever I was and whoever I met, and their attraction to me (simple attraction, not merely sexual) was inevitable. But it was what emanated from *me*, not what I got from *others*, that made them want to be around me.

Now to answer your question—how do you make your life more than being inconsequential? It begins by seeing yourself as consequential. Do you ever tell yourself that you're "just" a housewife with nothing to contribute outside of the home? Do you feel like you contribute less to society than someone who works outside the home and has regular adult interactions? **It begins by how you see yourself, and that self-perception radiates from you during your interactions with others.**

People want to feel better as a result of an interaction with someone else, not drained. Give, and you shall receive. Overflow and you shall have more friends than you can handle.

EIGHTY-NINE

Men with attractive girlfriends, how do you deal with the attention they may get?

So let me say that my girlfriend is very attractive. She gets hit on by guys every time she goes out with her girlfriends. We've been dating for two years now, and I battle with finding the attention she gets annoying, while it also makes me appreciate what I have.

My girlfriend is taking a trip to Vegas for the first time with her girlfriends, and the dresses she's shown me will turn heads. I feel insecure about this trip—not because I don't trust her, but I just don't trust all the random guys that could be approaching her at pool parties, clubs, bars, etc.

I'm trying to be levelheaded about this since I know she's dressing up because she's on vacation and with her girlfriends and they'll be going out to restaurants, bars, clubs—it's what you do, but her being in Vegas is kind of throwing me off.

How do you guys deal with the attention your significant other gets?

I deal with the attention my significant other gets with the confidence I have in our relationship, the quality I know I bring to the table, and my understanding of women.

You have reason to have confidence in your relationship. You've been with her for two years, and in that time, she hasn't been enticed to leave you by another man. She's attractive and she gets attention. If any of those guys had a chance of stealing her from you, they would've.

It's natural that she's going to be hit on by guys since she's beautiful! They're not blind, and it's in their nature to go after beautiful women. Count it as a compliment to both her and you instead of a threat to you. Know that what you give is so satisfying to her that she doesn't need to look elsewhere for it, and realize that, though women are attracted to good looking men, that's not as high on their list as it is for us. Men are much more visual creatures than women.

Think about the quality of what you give to the relationship versus what a man approaching her would promise. How can he compete with the breadth and depth of what you've given over two years in having one conversation with her? Even if he promised her the moon and the stars (which he cannot give) or something he *could* give, like material things, how does that compare with the intangible seeds you've planted in your relationship with her that have blossomed over time?

Here are some things to understand about women. A more attractive woman doesn't require more love than a less attractive one, and every one of them is looking for love—real, deep, sincere, faithful love. One of the reasons I'm not intimidated to approach a beautiful and successful woman is because I know she needs real love as much as anyone else does. Even if she says no, it's her loss, because I know what she's missing out on, as I know what I have to give and how rare it is.

And I'm not simply talking about looks, muscles, or size—I'm talking about things that last long after those things diminish.

Also, I'm not sure if you've heard the saying, but I've found it to be true: women don't dress for men—they dress for other women. You said she's going to Vegas with her girlfriends. It makes sense that she'd wear head-turning dresses. Her girlfriends will, too, and they'll compliment. each other on how cute they look. On the other hand, what does a man do when he sees a woman in a head-turning dress? He usually imagines it *off* her more than he admires it *on* her.

Believe in yourself and what you give to the relationship. Understand that it has lasted two years for a reason. Be happy for her to be with her girlfriends in Vegas, tell her so, excitedly ask her about and listen to her describe the trip when she returns, and be ready to reap the rewards!

NINETY

I met someone I like more than my wife.

I *have so much in common with her, and I can't get her out of my head.*

I feel a sense of awe for who she is, and it's difficult to articulate, but I just never thought I'd meet someone like her.

Maybe I should just be grateful to know her and keep this to myself. She lives a couple of states away from me, and I have no idea how she feels about me. I think I've gotten signs from her like she's attracted to me, but then I question whether it's wishful thinking.

Tell me to stop dreaming and just deal with it. Please. I fear that I'd mess up too much if I did anything to pursue this.

What are you supposed to do? It's such a horrible thing to try to talk about.

The worst thing you can do is try to bury your thoughts because they make you feel guilty. The more you fight these things you're thinking, the more trouble you'll have dealing with them. Acting like you don't feel what you feel won't make the feelings go away. Lying to yourself will only make it worse, and you'll have less ability to keep from giving in to the feelings when you try to pretend they don't exist. Shaming yourself for these thoughts is another way of saying that these thoughts are more powerful than you. How can that be true when the thoughts *are* you?

You *can* feel these things without pursuing them—in fact, it's best to acknowledge what's going on inside of you. Just acknowledge it without doing anything about it. Whenever the thoughts come up or the feelings arise, accept their presence, and continue doing whatever it was you were doing before the thoughts and feelings arose.

What'll happen when you do this?

The novelty of the thoughts and feelings will begin to subside. Though they seem to overwhelm your sense of loyalty now, the tables will turn over time. And I say seem because, as threatening as they appear to be to your relationship with your wife, it's obvious that your devotion to that relationship is enough to keep you from actively pursuing anything with this other person.

At the same time, talk to yourself whenever you find yourself wishing that your wife had the same qualities as this other woman. Remind yourself why you fell in love with your wife. Remember and appreciate her good qualities. Remind yourself why you don't want to mess up your relationship with her.

You can experience both feelings at the same time, and you should allow yourself to do so, since you already are. In the end, if you do nothing else about the feelings for this other woman than experience them and let them pass, they'll lose their power.

NINETY-ONE

I think my husband is going to leave me. What do I do?

*M*y husband and I have been married for ten years next week, and together for thirteen years. During this time, I've had cancer (nine years cancer free!) and have become disabled (unrelated to cancer). I'm an ambulatory wheelchair user, so I can walk a little, but use a wheelchair when out of the house.

Recently, my husband has been quite withdrawn. He started de-cluttering and bought his own laptop (we've previously shared one). On Monday, he asked me what was up, as I seemed sad. I very bravely said that I thought he might be planning to leave me based on his actions.

He didn't deny it.

He said he's really struggling with things at the moment, that he's not good enough for me, and that I should be with someone who'll take care of me properly. I'm honestly so confused because he's been so amazing up until quite recently. He deals with a lot of things around the house, including laundry and cooking.

We're going away for our anniversary next week and he seems to think that being away will sort everything out, but I'm not sure. I honestly dread it now.

I'd really appreciate any advice you could give me on how I should proceed or which questions I should ask him to try to get to the bottom of things.

Thanks in advance.

I can understand why his behavior would seem confusing. While he takes care of you and things around the house, he's withdrawing. He's gotten his own laptop. He doesn't believe he's good enough for you and thinks you should be with someone who'll take care of you properly.

I have a few suggestions for questions you should ask.

Ask him what he's done that he feels guilty about. Ask him if he's gotten his own laptop to watch pornography. Ask him if there's someone else. Have a frank discussion about why he feels he's not good enough for you.

Please allow me to explain why I suggest these questions, while providing this disclaimer: I don't propose these questions because he's guilty of anything, so don't approach this as if you're accusing him of these things—rather, that you genuinely want to know what's going on, and you're concerned about things.

When someone believes they're not good enough for you when their behavior towards you has demonstrated otherwise, chances are that person has done something you don't know about for which they feel guilty and it's eating them up inside.

It's possible that he got his own laptop so that you wouldn't accidentally (or purposefully) go through his viewing history. That could be the case if he's looking at something he doesn't want you to know about, like pornography, or contacting someone via a dating site that he doesn't want you to know about. This would also explain his guilty feeling and why he thinks he's not good enough for you.

If he's already involved with someone else while telling himself you don't deserve to be cheated on, he may go through extra efforts taking care of you to ease his conscience while also withdrawing from you.

What does he think going away will sort out? If he's done something for which he feels guilty, he may think that going away together will prevent him from engaging in that behavior, thus easing his guilt, and may rekindle feelings he had for you.

While you may dread finding out whatever's at the bottom of his behavior, it's better to know than to live in blissful ignorance, isn't it? Don't try to get rid of that feeling before you ask the questions—**feel the dread and do it anyway.**

NINETY-TWO

I feel financially overwhelmed paying all the house bills for my dad when my siblings won't help, too.

I'm a young man with a steady job, making a decent wage for **myself**. *I still live at home and was planning to move out with my significant other soon. I also have a sibling ten years older than me who lives in the same home.*

My dad, head of the household, is unable to work anymore due to a disability and is in the process of getting pension benefits, but it's a long process. Everyone relies on me to pay all the bills, which add up to over $3,000 a month.

I'm trying to progress in life and move forward but I can't do so because I feel that I must help them. I'm drowning trying to support an entire household and trying to take care of my own things.

What should I do? I've brought this up to my other siblings and it seems like they have no intention of helping.

Recognize how it got to this point. Though this may not be the exact scenario, allow me to recreate what may have happened.

A bill became due (or overdue), and either you watched your father worry about how it was going to be paid, or he let the people in the house know that he was worried about how it would be paid. He then either asked for help or, more likely, you offered to help. This was done out the kindness of your heart and your love and appreciation for your father. He agreed to let you help, and you paid the bill. This repeated itself bill by bill until, seeing that his pension benefits were taking longer than you anticipated, you ended up with all the bills.

In the meantime, your sibling didn't step up to help, and you haven't flat out asked them to help. When you brought it up, you didn't ask them for help; you waited for them to offer to help, and they didn't.

I have two suggestions. The first is to ask your sibling if they'd take some of the bills as their responsibility. **Let them know that it's not fair for them to live in the house with you and accept none of the responsibility that comes with it.** It would be best to have this conversation in a meeting with both your sibling and your father present. While it may be easier for them to ignore your request if you approach them one on one, it may be harder for them to do the same when they're in front of your father.

The second suggestion is for you to decide to move out in, say, six months (or three months or one month or whatever timeframe you prefer). Let your family know the plan and remind them that it gives them plenty of time to make other arrangements to take care of the household expenses. Then stick to the plan, gently giving a countdown every now and then until you leave. It gives them plenty of time to come up with another means to pay the bills and as you remind them with your countdown that you're leaving, it'll show them that you're serious about moving out.

(By the way, there's nothing wrong with deciding to follow *both* suggestions!)

NINETY-THREE

What does a healthy marriage feel like?

I grew up in a dysfunctional family. I had nowhere to learn what love should be like in a marriage. I've watched films, seen social media posts of perfect marriages, etc., but it just doesn't seem true.

I sometimes wonder: what's a normal marriage like? Do you always smile when you look at each other? Do you sometimes get tired of the other person? Do you sometimes imagine your life going differently? Are you in love?

I understand, as I also grew up in a dysfunctional family. We often daydream about the best parts of relationships, fueled by things like films, Hallmark movies, and social media posts, but you correctly realized that these often-idealized versions of relationships aren't how they really are. Unfortunately, many remain frustrated because things aren't how they seem in these exaggeratedly romanticized flicks.

A "normal" marriage is, in many ways, an extension of life itself. Like life, it contains triumph and tragedy, heartache and happiness, pleasure and pain. There are moments when you smile at each other, and there are moments when you take each other for granted, just as there are moments when you walk outside with a thousand things on your mind, oblivious to your surroundings, while there are other moments when you sit with nature and bask in its glorious beauty or appreciate the peace of the ebb and flow of life with the one you love.

What people describe as "getting tired of the other person" is usually either becoming frustrated with one or more of their behaviors or just your own temporary need to be alone.

Like life itself, we look back over it and wonder how it would've been if things had happened differently in the past. Sometimes, people think the solution is to start over again and create a different past with someone else—something you can't do with life itself. That's a critical difference between a "normal" marriage and life.

You asked, "are you in love?" (I'm interpreting that question to sound like, "Is one who is in a healthy marriage also in love?") You are, but that means different things over time. In the beginning, it's "puppy love"—as intense a romantic attachment as it is shallow. I think of it as 10 miles wide and 1 inch deep. As time goes on and you move from puppy love to mature love, the width lessens while the depth increases. Much later, as you begin to really appreciate the person you're with instead of just assuming they'll always be there, the intensity begins to widen again while the depth continues to become even deeper. In this final growth, there is no end. To give and receive this type of love, though, you must be emotionally healed and whole.

I wish you this kind of final kind of love.

NINETY-FOUR

How do I make my friend comfortable in her last days?

My friend has Stage IV pancreatic cancer. She's in the hospital right now battling pneumonia and they don't know when they're going to send her home. Her whole body is shutting down at this point and as much as I want to hope she's going to pull through, I just don't know.

She doesn't have any family besides her boyfriend, who can't take time off from work to take care of her. She's got two friends who still see her—the druggie neighbor who tries to bum/buy her pain meds, and me. She's struggling hard right now, not just with the pain and the cancer, but with the loneliness.

I visit her as much as I can, but what can I do to make her feel as loved and comfortable as I can?

You might want to talk with the hospital chaplain to see if s/he knows of any vetted volunteer patient visitor organizations.

Another idea is to get in touch with your local hospice program. They have helpers who will sit with people, even in shifts, to ensure they're not alone. They also have experience with the terminally ill, so they won't act awkward around your friend.

There is also a program called "No One Dies Alone," where compassionate volunteers provide visitation in three-hour shifts to ensure the patient is never alone. They talk to the patient, hold their hand, or just act as a caring presence for them.

Most of all, **I'm sure she appreciates your being there. Not because you have any professional experience, but because you love her.**

As you sit with her, as you talk to her, and as you in so many other ways love her, it makes her feel like there's something good left in the world she's slipping away from. I'm sure she appreciates your efforts, and your desire to see her so cared for, in more ways than she can express. Your love for her makes you wish you could do more, and your efforts to help ease her loneliness are acts that also reduce the sting from any feelings of helplessness you may have.

I remember the haunting conversation I had with my niece before she died, when she said to me, "Uncle Leonard, I'm scared." She didn't say why she was scared, but she didn't have to. I'm sure she was scared of the unknown. Scared of dying. Scared of being alone. Other family members and I sat with her in hospice for days, until her last heartbeat. We sang, we reminisced, we laughed, we cried.

I got to spend time with my sister a couple of weeks before she died. She cried as she told me, over and over, how appreciative she was that I was there. She didn't want to be too fussed over, but she felt and was acutely aware of the love that surrounded her by me and others. She asked me to give her eulogy, as did my mother, before she died. The grief while giving it was overcome by the honor of being asked to do it.

I say these things to say this—what you're doing for your friend right now is an honor and tribute to her life, and the more people you can enlist to be there for her, the greater the tribute.

NINETY-FIVE

Feeling suicidal because I'm not taken seriously enough in relationships. How do I feel better?

*W*oke up this morning in tears. Resorted to cutting myself right away to ease the tears.

I want to know what I should do for a guy to take me seriously in relationships and to not be seen as some sex object. I'm fed up and want to overcome this. Ever since my first heartbreak at 14 and then being emotionally manipulated into sex at the age of 15, I've tried to do better and improve myself.

I did a complete 180 on everything and there's still nothing. Looks? I try to look polished and well dressed on the regular. Career? I'm only one semester away from completing my degree. Interests? Over the years I've picked up a liking for photography, F1, watches, and learned a bit of politics in my country to brush up on having small conversations. Still nothing. I feel ugly and insecure that no one wants to be with me or make it official when it comes to relationships.

I feel worthless. If anything, when it comes to sex, I've had so many men that wanted to do it with me, and it makes me feel sick to my stomach. I just want someone to ask me about my day and care about me. I don't know what I'm doing wrong, and I'd like to know. I want to be girlfriend material and the kind of person a guy wouldn't mind showing off to his friends and family. It's like there's no benefit to all the effort I put into myself, and I feel worn out.

I see my friends get into these loving relationships effortlessly and I wish I was them. Please help me out. How does one change this? How do you even love yourself when you have a history of getting bullied? Why can't I have better in life? Why is it that when you're unhappy everyone treats you so badly? Just why?

I believe the answers to your questions are contained in something you said about yourself: "I feel worthless." If you believe yourself worthless, how will you believe someone else can find you worthwhile?

This could very well have begun during those periods when you were bullied. I'm sure that, as part of that bullying, you were called names and belittled. You were probably made to feel like you were worthless. You might've even been told that you may as well kill yourself, as you weren't worth the air others breathed. As damaging as these things are, they're less damaging than when we start to believe and say these things about ourselves.

To be considered worthwhile by others, you must first consider yourself worthwhile. You must believe it with every fiber of your being. But how, you may ask, do you get there?

First, let's talk about what hasn't worked. Changing the way you look without changing the way you think about yourself. Finding outside interests without finding yourself interesting. Wanting a man to care about you without caring how you think of yourself. Working to be girlfriend material without working to be self-friend material. Cutting yourself.

Now let's talk about what will work.

You see your friends having loving relationships effortlessly. How does this happen?

Because they believe themselves worthy of these relationships, apart from how they dress, what hobbies they have, their level of education, or their interests. They believe themselves girlfriend material, not just sexual objects.

The way you dress should reflect how you already feel about yourself, not just as a way to attract men. Your interests should be *your* interests, not a way to make you seem more interesting. Your career should reflect your passion, not an attempt to seem worthwhile.

This goes back to learning to love yourself. I often ask this question: if you don't love yourself, how can you expect others to love you? **If you can come up with reasons you aren't worth self-love, aren't those same reasons good enough to keep others from loving you?**

If you learn to love yourself, however, it will attract others' love. If you believe yourself worthwhile, others will find you worthwhile.

Begin by challenging the things that the bullies said to you. If they said you were worthless, ask yourself how they came up with that assessment. I'm sure you won't be able to think of a reason why what they said was true. It was just hurting people hurting other people. Once you decide that they had no real reason to conclude you're worthless, ask yourself why you started believing what they said. Because so many of them said it? Because they said it so often? Do either of those things make it true?

Once you decide that what they said isn't true, tell yourself you're worth unconditionally loving yourself. Place stickers around your room reminding yourself of that fact. The more we tell ourselves negative things about ourselves, the deeper they imprint in our minds. To change this, we must repeatedly tell ourselves positive things about ourselves, even if we don't believe what we're saying at first. I promise you that you didn't believe your bullies the first time they belittled you, but over time, you did. It's the same with believing good things about yourself now.

This is how you feel better. You relearn to love yourself. You remind yourself that you're worthwhile, that you're wonderful, that you've got a lot to offer, that you're a person with hopes and dreams worth fulfilling.

I want to emphasize what I said earlier (and even make it more specific) because it's so important: when you learn to love yourself, you'll attract true love.

NINETY-SIX

I want to be a better person. How do I do it?

To keep it short, I'm always stressed about my relationship because we argue a lot, my living status because I'm poor/homeless, and my friends because they seem fake. I want to be positive no matter the situation because I'm so pessimistic, and I feel like I should enjoy life no matter what, but I don't know how to get out of this negative thought loop.

How do I start? How do I stay consistent? What's a good plan?

People who spend time in negative thought loops usually have the idea that, if they think/expect the worst, if the worst doesn't happen, they'll feel better, and if it does, they won't be caught off guard. This is a warped version of the ancient Stoic practice of *premeditatio malorum*.

Premeditatio malorum (premeditation of the bad) is the practice of imagining worst-case scenarios, but it's for the purpose of creating solutions in case things *do* go wrong. **If you only imagine the worst without using that foreknowledge to prepare solutions, you'll become pessimistic.** Pessimism is problem-focused, whereas premeditatio malorum is solution-focused.

A good plan would be to turn pessimism into premeditatio malorum. Let's practice.

Your living status is poor/homeless. Instead of focusing on things as they are, what are some ways that you can turn that around? Realize it'll take some time, but can you get a better job? Can you train for a better position?

You argue a lot in your relationship. What are the things you argue about? Does it end up being two or three particular things, no matter how it starts? List the things that you argue about the most by how often you argue about them, with the one most argued about being at the top of the list. Tackle those things one at a time. What can you *do* about it? What are you willing to do about it, and what are you unwilling to do about it? Have a conversation about it when you both are in a relatively good mood, with the purpose of coming up with solutions.

Your friends seem fake. Why? Is it because they look for the good in things? They don't see things the way you've been seeing them? Or is there another reason? Do you have proof they've been fake? Is it possible to give them the benefit of the doubt?

What law says you must always be positive no matter what the situation? There's no such law. In fact, it's unrealistic to always enjoy life, no matter what. The key is to have a way to see the light at the end of the tunnel, the sunshine after the gloomy sky, and know that life contains both sadness and happiness, joy and pain, sunshine and rain, and appreciate what both teach. It's as unrealistic to always be optimistic as it is to always be pessimistic. The key is to become *omnimistic*—that is, allow the premeditatio malorum of pessimism to work together with the solution-focused response of optimism.

NINETY-SEVEN

How do you gain clarity or heal your inner wounds to move forward?

I was wondering how to deal with the constant pains and re-grets about past actions. Wondering or thinking about how things should've been. Wondering "what if" or wondering why I didn't do this or that sooner. If I had known then what I know now then, the outcome would've been different.

I find myself chasing after what's long gone, something that's not there anymore. What once was but isn't anymore. Coming to terms with the fact that it's gone.

How do you gain clarity and come to terms with your past?

Are the things you regret things you can change? If they're things that happened in the past, I know that the answer is no.

If any of us had the power to change the past, I'm sure there'd be something we'd love to change. As we don't have that power, what positive thing comes from wishing we did? I want you to really think about this question. **What *positive* thing comes from wishing we could change the past?** The answer is that there's *no* positive thing that comes from wishing we could change the past. Since there's no positive thing that comes from wishing we had a power we don't, nor can have, why continue to wish for it and set ourselves up for continual frustration, depression, regret, and insanity? And when I mention insanity here, I'm referring to the quote attributed to Albert Einstein: insanity is doing the same thing over and over again (in this case, wishing you could change the past) expecting a different result.

Once you gain clarity on that, it's time to heal your inner wounds. This is how you do it—tell yourself that, had you known better, you would've done better. Repeat that again and again, especially when you feel despair about things you did in the past, until you feel better. Realize that you'll continue to cycle between feeling better and falling back into despair, and don't beat yourself up for feeling the despair, but repeat that mantra to yourself: had you known better, you would've done better. Then resolve not to make the same mistakes and keep that promise to yourself the best you can. When you fail, remind yourself that the mistake is now in your past and there's nothing you can do to change it.

Also remind yourself that you can't find what isn't there whenever you're tempted to chase after what's long gone. Accept that it's gone, and you'll learn to come to terms with the fact that it's gone, as acceptance is necessary before coming to terms. As long as you say to yourself "but...but..." you won't accept it, and if you won't accept it, you won't come to terms with it.

NINETY-EIGHT

What do you do when you wish something bad would happen to you just so someone else would notice/care?

Y ou realize that, if it takes something bad happening to you to get people to come around, show you attention, and act as if they care, there's a reason they're not doing those things now, and that reason has something to do with you. If everyone's acting this way toward you, *everyone's* not the problem—*you* are the common denominator.

I'm not trying to be mean or insensitive but am attempting to get to the root of the matter.

What is it about you that keeps others away? Have you shown care to others without giving the impression that you're looking for something from it as a result? Have you shown selfishness when it comes to love, only giving it to those who first give it to you and withholding it from those who don't? Do you complain a lot and are otherwise negative in your conversations with others? Do you mope about in a depressed state, focusing on yourself and your problems and hoping others will take notice and show concern?

Once you figure out what it is that you do which keeps others away, focus on changing that behavior (or those behaviors). Instead of wishing something bad would happen to you, use that energy to focus on being for others what you want them to be for you. You want others to care about you? Care about them. You want others to listen to you? Listen to them. You want others to notice you? Notice them. You want others to show you love? Show them love. Don't just do these things until you get what you want, but do them all the time, and your heart won't believe that it has the room to receive all that will be given back to you.

NINETY-NINE

Is self-acceptance the first step to work on to improve yourself?

*L*ike does self-acceptance come first, even before self-esteem, self-worth, or self-confidence?

Yes, it begins with self-acceptance. While self-acceptance is one's acceptance of both positive and negative things about themselves, it doesn't attempt to justify or excuse the negative things. It understands that no one's perfect, we all have flaws, and you accept yourself—flaws and all—while you work on those flaws, which will be a lifelong endeavor. When you accept yourself, you believe you're worthy of love yourself despite your shortcomings, instead of thinking you must be perfect to be worthy of loving yourself.

This self-acceptance then creates a sense of self-worth. If you believe you're good enough to love and accept yourself, you'll believe you're good enough to accept love and a sense of belonging from others. **If we don't truly love ourselves, we'll reject true love from others.**

If we don't truly accept ourselves, we'll reject being truly accepted by others.

Once you love and accept yourself and accept love and a sense of belonging from others, you gain the confidence in your worth that self-esteem brings. You respect yourself and are confident in both your worth and your abilities.

From there, you'll be able to trust your abilities, qualities, and judgment with self-confidence. You'll have a sense of control over your life and trust your ability to navigate decisions. Your goals will be realistic, as will your expectations, you'll be able to say what you want without feeling the need to be aggressive, and you'll be able to handle criticism without taking it personally.

How do I care less about other people?

I'm hyperaware of my surroundings. Like I always step aside for others on sidewalks to let other people pass. I always hurry up at the supermarket. I'm always afraid to make people feel uncomfortable or upset.

What can I do to get an "I don't care" attitude?

One of the ways we attempt to remedy an extreme in one direction is by finding a way to move to an extreme in the opposite direction. Be careful of that. One end of your extreme is being afraid to make other people feel uncomfortable or upset, while the other extreme is to have an "I don't care" attitude. The best thing to do is to find the middle ground between the two.

And how do you do that? By challenging your belief. Which belief is that? The belief that you must be careful to make sure you don't make people feel uncomfortable or upset.

Here's how you challenge it.

How do you *make* people uncomfortable or upset? Do you *force* them to become uncomfortable or upset? Do you have the power to force anyone to feel anything? Even if you held a gun up to their head and told them to feel something—anything—or die, it would still be their choice to feel that thing rather than to die.

You think people must like you and approve of you and your actions, and you think it's catastrophic when they don't. But the reality is this: it's impossible to make everyone like you. In fact, **you don't always like yourself, so how can it be realistic to expect everyone else to always like you?** If you *must* have other people's approval, you'll always be doing things *they* like, which means that there'll be times you won't be doing things *you* like just because you're looking for others' approval. **If you try too hard to get other people to like you, you'll lose their respect.**

Instead of thinking about how awful it is that everyone doesn't like you, think this instead: 'It would be *nice* if everyone liked me, but that's not reality. In the real world, I won't always be liked, and that's okay because that's life, and besides, in the real world I don't always like myself.' It may not feel good to think that not everyone likes you, but it's not the end of the world, and it won't kill you.

As you practice thinking this way instead of assuming you're responsible for everyone else's happiness, you'll loosen up, you'll be less concerned about making others uncomfortable or upset, and you'll be a happier person. You won't need an "I don't care" attitude, because you'll realize that you don't have to stop caring to understand that the world's comfort has never been assigned as your responsibility. Until a big, booming voice from the heavens declare you the one person responsible for the comfort and happiness of others, don't try to assume that obligation.

The middle ground turns "I must make sure everyone likes me" into "it would be nice if everyone liked me, but it's unrealistic, so I won't expect it." There's an awful sense of hopelessness in the first statement, but an incredible sense of freedom in the second one!

About the Author

Leonard Adams was trained as a United States Army counselor in 1981, using a multimodal therapeutic approach. In that capacity, he performed individual, marital, and family counseling, as well as hospice counseling, rape and crisis intervention, and conducted anger management classes. In addition, as a counselor for the Tennesse State prison system, he performed counseling services at a hospital prison, at a classification prison, and on Death Row. He also trained counselors and correctional officers for the State of Tennessee through the Tennessee Correction Academy, and taught college-level counseling courses in Hawaii through the Word of Life Institute.

More information can be found at https://www.relearninglove.com.

Printed in the USA
CPSIA information can be obtained
at www.ICGtesting.com
LVHW011058270824
789418LV00021B/276